PLAY LIKE

chelsea fc

Words: Dominic Bliss
Design: Jamie Dunmore
Production: Adam Oldfield

Produced by Sport Media, Trinity Mirror North West

Executive Editor: Ken Rogers. Senior Editor: Steve Hanrahan
Senior Production Editor: Paul Dove. Senior Art Editor: Rick Cooke
Sub Editor: Gary Gilliland
Chelsea Magazine/Programme Editor: David Antill
Writers: Dominic Bliss, Richard Godden, James Sugrue
Designers: Glen Hind, James Kenyon

Business Development Director: Mark Dickinson
Sales and Marketing Manager: Elizabeth Morgan
Sales and Marketing Assistant: Karen Cadman
Business Development Manager: Sarah Woodley-Dyne
Account Managers: Thomas Peck, Simon Ellis

ISBN: 9781906802615

Photographs: Darren Walsh, Chelsea FC, Trinity Mirror, Getty Images, PA Photos.
Printed in Slovenia by arrangement with KINT Ljubljana

CARLO
ANCELOTTI

Perhaps, by reading this book, and by watching us play, the enthusiasm this squad has for football will transfer to you

I grew to love football as a boy from watching the great Inter Milan side of the 1960s, who won title after title, both in Italy and in Europe. They were a great side, whose star player was my hero Sandro Mazzola, a wonderfully skilful forward who could dribble the ball with fantastic ability.

Since then I have enjoyed playing the game from youth level, through to Serie A, where I represented Roma and AC Milan, and learned from some of the best players and coaches in the game.

I have also been fortunate to coach some great teams since then and I hope this Chelsea team can have the same impact on young footballers as the Inter side I supported had on me.

Perhaps, by reading this book, and by watching us play, the enthusiasm this squad has for football will transfer to you.

JOHN TERRY

When kids are still at a young age, I think it's important for parents and coaches to make it fun

I used to play football as much as I possibly could when I was a youngster and I remember just having that excitement about playing all the time. I came to Chelsea as a teenager and we had a coach called Bob Osborn at Under-14s, who's still here actually - he just said to us, go out there and show me what you can do.

That sort of advice gets you feeling confident about yourself and your ability when you're younger and I would point to that as a good example. When kids are still at a young age, I think it's important for parents and coaches to make it fun and you'll start learning more serious parts of the game and positional stuff as you get older.

It's also important to put in the hours if you want to make the most of your talent. I'll always remember when I was first coming into the senior fold here how impressed I was with Gianfranco Zola and his commitment as well. He was coming to the end of his career, had shown everyone what a great player he was, but he still did everything right - trained hard, ate well and stayed behind to do extra work afterwards.

Hopefully, the Chelsea players in this squad, who have contributed to this book, can drive young players forward in the same way.

FRANK
LAMPARD

Once you get involved in the game it becomes a part of your life

I was born into football in my family. From a very young age, my dad, my uncle and then my cousins were footballers, so that inspired me to try and do the same.

I remember my dad taking me over the park to join this team and it was just a walk from my house. We just sort of gatecrashed training one day, my dad spoke to the manager and I remember playing a bit of five-a-side. I scored an own goal actually - I got a bit excited, got passed the ball and hit it in my own net!

But once you get involved in the game it becomes a part of your life. I worked hard all through my childhood and my youth team days to make the best of myself and that has never stopped. Even though there were times when I thought some of the other kids were better than me, I never gave up working on my stamina, my passing, my touch - everything.

I saw many a player, some of whom were probably better than me at the time who, by the time we got the youth team, hadn't developed for whatever reason or they got other interests and didn't make it in football. At the end of the day I wanted it a lot more than they did and I think that's the most important thing.

DIDIER
DROGBA

If the passion I have comes through on the pages of this book, then I hope it will inspire new players to enjoy the game that I love

Football has always been so important to me, from when I was a boy it has dictated much of my life. I moved from my home in Ivory Coast to be with my uncle, Michel Goba, who was a professional footballer himself in France.

That move made it possible for me to become a footballer and I learned from him, as well as the many coaches I had across the country when I followed my uncle from club to club.

One coach in particular - Jean Trechet - was important in teaching me, when I was about 11, to have passion of playing, not just in winning or losing, but just for playing and enjoying being with my friends.

If the passion I have - and I know my team-mates feel it too - comes through on the pages of this book, then I hope it will inspire new players to enjoy the game that I love.

CONTENTS

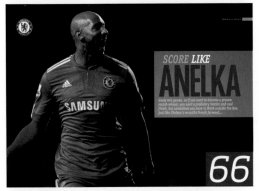

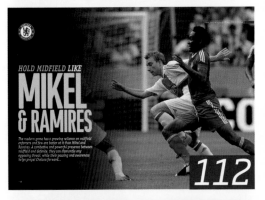

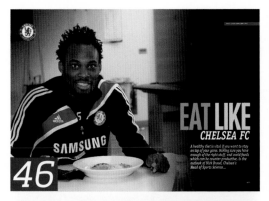

EAT LIKE
CHELSEA FC

A healthy diet is vital if you want to stay on top of your game. Making sure you have enough of the right stuff, and avoid foods which can be counter-productive, is the outlook of Nick Broad, Chelsea's Head of Sports Science...

46

SCORE *LIKE*
DROGBA

Chelsea's number 11 has proved a prolific goalscorer over the years, but it takes a lot more than just good finishing to be considered a top striker. Here's where you can learn from the best...

56

ATTACK *LIKE*
KALOU
& BENAYOUN

Whether you're running at defenders, creating space with your movement, or making a key assist, it's important to provide support to your front line. As an attack-minded midfielder, or auxiliary forward, you can also benefit from a fair share of goals by following the model of Salomon Kalou and Yossi Benayoun...

88

PLAY *LIKE*
LAMPARD

Every successful team needs an inspirational figure. Someone capable of covering the whole pitch, scoring crucial goals and providing key assists. Frank Lampard has been that man at Chelsea for almost a decade. Here's how...

98

DEFEND *LIKE*
TERRY

English centre-halves are regarded as some of the most robust and commanding figures in football. Brave, committed and a reassuring influence on the whole team, some come more imposing than John Terry, a leader on and off the field...

136

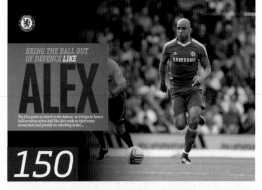

BRING THE BALL OUT
OF DEFENCE *LIKE*
ALEX

The first point of attack is the defence, so it helps to have a ball-carrying centre-half like Alex ready to inject some momentum and provide an attacking outlet.

150

MANAGE *LIKE*
ANCELOTTI

You've seen what it takes to become a Chelsea player, but how do you get the best out of them when it matters most? Carlo Ancelotti has a track record of success in management and here's how he does it...

184

THINK LIKE
CHELSEA FC

A player's talent is the thing that comes first and foremost in everyone's mind with a young footballer. but, as Chelsea assistant manager Ray Wilkins explains, there are so many more things that you need to have in your armoury to achieve greatness or to achieve status as a Premier League footballer...

196

TRAIN LIKE
CHELSEA FC

It takes a lot of planning off the field to ensure the success Chelsea have on it. The importance of training hard reflects on your performance, which is why assistant first team coach Paul Clement, along with the other club coaches, puts a lot of effort into ensuring the team reach their full potential on matchdays...

PAUL CLEMENT SAYS...

Advanced planning

The first part of planning training is drawing up a monthly schedule. We're a very busy club, taking part in a lot of competitions - the Premier League, the UEFA Champions League, the FA Cup and the Carling Cup - and the majority of our first-team squad are internationals as well, either at senior level or with the Under-21s. So a monthly schedule can end up looking very busy.

Once we know where all the fixtures are going to fit in, we plan our training schedule one month in advance. The first things to go on the schedule are the dates of all our fixtures for that month and, once you've done that, you're able to put down the times and dates of training sessions and, if any, the free days.

But in a month where your players are competing in the Premier League, the Champions

League, the Carling Cup and at international level, days off are few and far between. Whereas when you're able to train solidly from weekend to weekend, you're sometimes able to schedule a day off at some point during the week. These schedules are useful because players also have to organise their lives outside football, so we like to get it done in advance and put it up on the notice board so they can see what they have coming up.

Once we've done that, we plan the weekly training schedule, where we start going into more detail about what we'll do day-to-day, physically, technically and tactically. The content of training depends on whether we have games in midweek and whether we play on Saturday or Sunday each weekend.

Playing in numerous competitions all over Europe requires a lot of detail in the planning of training and recovery

Daily planning

Initially we'll have a meeting in the morning where the doctor and the medical department will provide information to the technical staff about who is available for training and who is not, as well as if any players need their training to be adapted for any reason. Once we have that information, the technical department then liaises with the sports science department about loading, what the specific physical emphasis will be on that particular day.

When all that information is available, Carlo will lead another discussion with myself, Ray Wilkins and the goalkeeper coach Christophe Lollichon about the structure and content of the session for that day.

A lot of preparation goes into planning training sessions and we regularly consult the medical and sports science departments

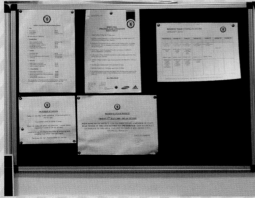

Training aims

In training, we work on the basics every day. We have very talented players who have a lot of qualities so it is important to use these strengths to the maximum. Putting players into formations and positions that suit their qualities places us in a strong position to go and win games. Tactical work (understanding the role in the team), as well as technical, physical and mental aspects, are developed and practiced during training sessions.

We also spend a lot of time looking at our opposition, through our scouting network and in video analysis in order to work out very clearly what their strengths and weaknesses are and what we will need to do in order to capitalise on that and win our games.

Typical training session

A typical training session will last from 45 minutes, which is the shortest duration, and 90 minutes. There is certainly an emphasis on working harder early mid-week and tapering off in the days closer to the game.

We would begin with a period of warming up, followed by a technical practice or a possession-based exercise, which usually work on passing and control. After that, our sports science staff run a physical exercise based on the theme and the requirements of that day's training.

There would then be a practice, which would work on either attacking, defending, transition (defence to attack, or attack to defence), duel-type exercises (such as one v one, two v two), even eleven-a-side if we're working on a specific tactical aspect. Then we would normally end with some kind of game with rules, either with or without goalkeepers, or a crossing and finishing session.

That summarises the structure of a typical session, within which we would obviously go into much more detail tailored to the situation with upcoming games.

Training always begins with
a warm-up session before
focusing on specific areas
of our game

Drill A :
Technical exercise

This is a passing exercise for 8-12 players, with four bases – two cones and two mannequins – forming a diamond. It develops passing, control and movement.

Beginning with two players on each base, the first player will pass the ball to the man at the base on his right and follow the pass on the run. The player receiving the pass will return the ball to the approaching man, who then pushes the ball through to the player at the base opposite his starting point. When this new player receives the ball, the move can begin again. This is particularly useful for co-ordinating simple passing movement.

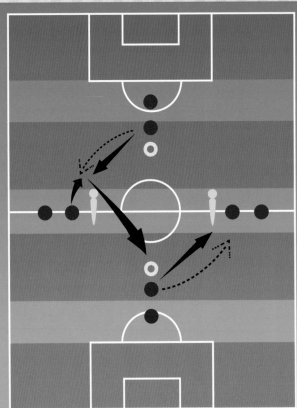

DRILL NOTES

■ **8 to 12 players**

■ **Develop passing, control, movement**

■ **Pass and follow to next position**

■ **Work on timing of movement**

Drill B :
Possession exercise

This is a an 8 vs 8 team exercise within an agreed playing area. Each team will have two additional 'target players' on the sides of the pitch who cannot enter the playing area. The ball is thrown into the square by the coach and the team in possession must keep the ball for as long as possible, using their two extra players on the sidelines to make the game effectively 10 vs 8 in their favour.

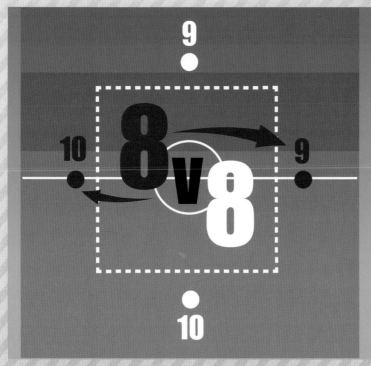

DRILL NOTES

■ **Two teams of 8**

■ **Additional two target players per team stood on the sides of the playing area**

■ **Retain possession for as long as possible**

Drill C : Combats
(2 v 2 on goal)

The first defender in line serves a long pass into the first attacker in the line diagonally opposite him. The attackers at the front of each line, then aim to combine together to score (using passes, overlaps, diagonal runs). The two defenders aim to push up following the initial long pass and, together with the goalkeeper, work to prevent goalscoring opportunities - this develops understanding of support, cover, communication, 1 vs 1 defending skills, blocking and tackling.

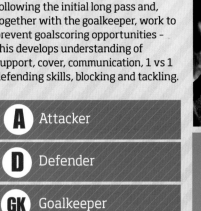

A Attacker

D Defender

GK Goalkeeper

DRILL NOTES

■ **Defender (D) serves a long pass into the attacker (A)**

■ **Attackers work together (passes, overlaps, diagonal runs) to score a goal**

■ **Defenders push up and work with the goalkeeper to prevent shooting opportunities (support, cover, communication, 1v1 defending and blocking)**

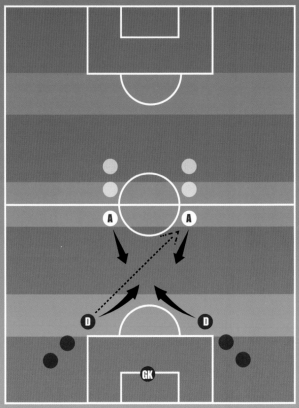

Drill D : Attacking exercise (counter-attacking)

This exercise pits four attacking players against three defenders to recreate a quick break or counter-attack situation which is likely to occur in a match. The coach serves the ball to the attacking players and they commence a fast-break attack. They will need to use overlaps or diagonal runs and switches of play to create a good shooting opportunity. This encourages your attackers to develop movement and speed of play.

C Coach

DRILL NOTES

■ **The coach (C) serves the ball to the attackers and they commence a fast break attack**

■ **Use overlaps, diagonal runs and switches of play to create goalscoring opportunities**

■ **Encourage movement and speed of play**

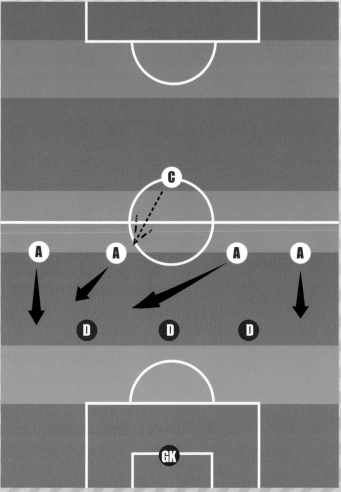

Drill E : **Defending exercise** (phase of play)

Begin with six attacking players and four defenders (to recreate a back four situation). Three attackers will represent a front three, while a fourth plays the role of a supporting midfielder and the other two attacking players are raiding full-backs. These attacking full-backs are encouraged to overlap with their wingers to create 2 vs 1 situations in wide areas, and also to attempt switches of play.

The defenders (organised as a back four) need to slide across the area together when the ball is switched to avoid gaps appearing and, in doing so, will strive to prevent goalscoring opportunities. This develops your defenders' communication, cover and support skills and also gives your attacking players practice against a more organised defensive set-up. You can progress to 6 vs 5 if you see fit.

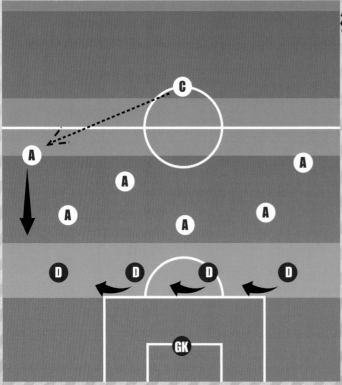

DRILL NOTES

■ **6 attackers v 4 defenders**

■ **Encourage the full-backs to overlap and create 2v1 situations in wide areas and switch the play**

■ **Back 4 (defenders) slide together when the ball is switched**

■ **Work on communication, cover and support**

■ **Progress to 6 v 5**

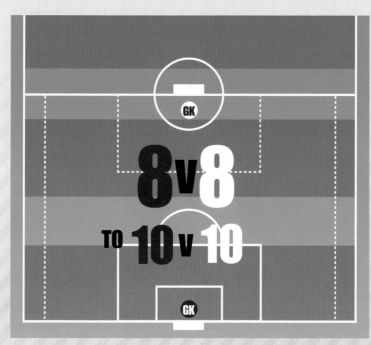

Drill F : Game with rules

Can be played with numbers from 8 vs 8 through to 10 vs 10 with goalkeepers using a half-pitch playing area and calling offsides only in the penalty area. You can then add specific rules to the game depending on what you want to work on that particular day, whether it be one or two-touches per player or just allowing free play..

DRILL NOTES

■ **Half pitch**

■ **8v8 to 10v10 with goalkeepers**

■ **Offsides in the penalty area**

■ **Condition from one touch to free play**

KEEP FIT LIKE
CHELSEA FC

Training regularly will help you stay fit, but it is important your body can cope with all aspects of the game, something first team fitness coach Glen Driscoll aims to drill into all of the players...

Glen Driscoll

Day-to-day role and scheduling

Each morning we hold a medical meeting at 8.30am. Individual requirements for players are discussed with fitness and science staff, but also with our doctors and physiotherapists as their perspective is invaluable. Having been a physiotherapist in the past, I really appreciate how important this link is and Thierry Laurent, Jason Palmer and Jon Fearn – our first team physiotherapists – have a wealth of experience.

The manager's meeting is held at 9.00am and Carlo holds court here! At this point, we have already planned the days' training – usually one week in advance during the season – but details of the session can be highlighted here.

Nick Broad, the club's Head of Science, will have scrolled through our large database to provide information on what the day's session will provide the players in a number of scientific areas. This is vital information because control of the football work helps us to periodise the week so the players get good intensity when appropriate but are also well recovered and prepared for optimum readiness leading up to a game. This is science applied to football, but it wouldn't be possible if the players didn't comply to wearing the GPS units and heart rate monitors every day.

After this, usually about 10.00am, myself, Ray Wilkins and Paul Clement prepare to set up the training pitches so the players can walk out to an organised field. Usually, two pitches are used and there is an organised strategy or rhythm to the training so players are not waiting around between drills. Again, this is important for providing a level of training intensity that replicates matches.

GPS units help monitor the players and provide useful data

Before training

Prior to training, players are encouraged to follow their individual injury-prevention programmes, which most often take place in the gym, but can also involve exercising in water or sand.

Other players may choose to visit our therapists and masseurs if appropriate. We are lucky we have a large, integrated team so that one-to-one supervision of players is the norm at Chelsea.

Chris Jones, Giovanni Mauri and Jon Fearn provide a lot of the active individual interventions whereas the work in the physio room is more passive. Immediately before training the science team equip the players with GPS and heart-rate technology to help monitor training.

Training

Training will typically take place between 11am and 12.30pm and warm-up, usually with myself, is mandatory. However, the rest of the session will depend on where we are in relation to the game. Even the warm-up content is dependent on the physical content of the session ahead. Each day will include a football-specific drill from myself, with a physical bias. This is to ensure the players are getting all the physical requirements they need.

STRETCH TIP...

QUADS: Pulling your legs back will help stretch the quadriceps, and stretching with a friend or team-mate can help you balance. The 'quads' are four muscles on the front of the thigh and are the strongest muscles in the human body.

If you don't feel a stretch in the front of your thigh, pull your foot further back and push your foot down into your palm.

CALVES: Place your hands on your team-mates' shoulders.

Step back with your right leg, keeping it straight, while the left knee bends. With both heels on the floor, lean forward by bending your left knee until you feel a stretch in your calf. Hold. Repeat on the other side.

HAMSTRINGS: Place right leg straight out in front of you while the left knee stays on the floor. Keep the right knee straight during the stretch. Keep the arch in your back as you reach to touch your toes, and pull them towards you. Repeat with the other side.

GROIN: You can stretch your groin and hamstring at the same time by kicking your leg high in the air and pressing down on your knee.

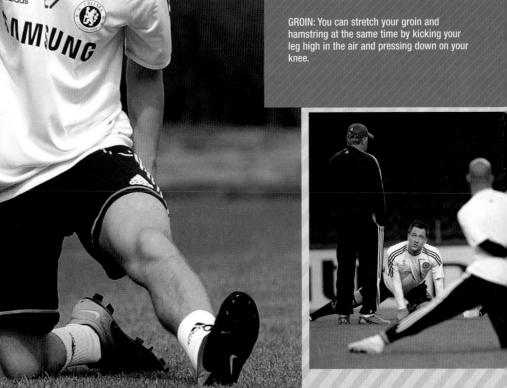

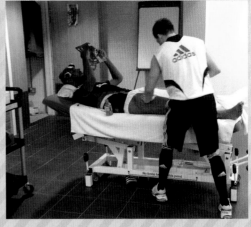

Recovery and refuelling

After training, recovery begins when the players refuel and replenish fluids. Ice-bathing and active cool downs are then performed as appropriate, while some players have a massage post-session. All players will then have lunch at 1.00pm.

During pre-season, the players will rest after lunch before the whole process is repeated for a second training session at 4.00pm.

Technology

Real-time monitoring technology allows us to assess the training intensity as it happens. As a player works, we can see the speed he hits, the distance he covers or the workload he undertakes. Carlo has embraced this and will regularly ask for feedback – typically he will ask the following:

● *Is the session on target for what we planned?*

● *Does the session need to be modified or cut short to protect players from fatigue, or optimise readiness for the next game?*

Drills emphasise the power and intensity of a match

Difference each drill makes to a player's fitness

In terms of fitness and conditioning, we have a global football philosophy at Chelsea. Basically, we get the players fit through football drills by changing the numbers, spaces and rules of the drills to obtain our objectives. To get aerobically fit the players don't run around pitches or cross country like in the old days, they play football. In fact, our GPS data tells us that players may cover over 8,000 metres in certain sessions, so to suggest that football training doesn't involve running is wrong, it is just more specific and therefore better conditions players to cope with the demands of matches.

Also, to develop strength, the players don't lift heavy weights in the gym, they perform football drills designed to emphasise player-to-player contact, power and high intensity accelerations and decelerations.

The drills I include daily will be football specific, but will be designed to get all the remaining physical requirements necessary to complete the players' conditioning. There is always a football component – the more the players enjoy training, the better the intensities we get out of them.

Box to box

A very intense drill designed to deliver the combined qualities of a short and sharp small-sided game after a transitional run. In this drill, if some players take too long (more than 15 seconds) to switch boxes, the game resumes and they potentially leave their team-mates 2 against 4. Just like a real match, individuals work hard for the team. Specific fitness conditioning like this allows players to maintain their technique and sharpness after fatiguing runs during a match.

Two 45-second 4v4 games, then 15 seconds for players to switch from box to box before resuming their game. Repeat the switch four times.

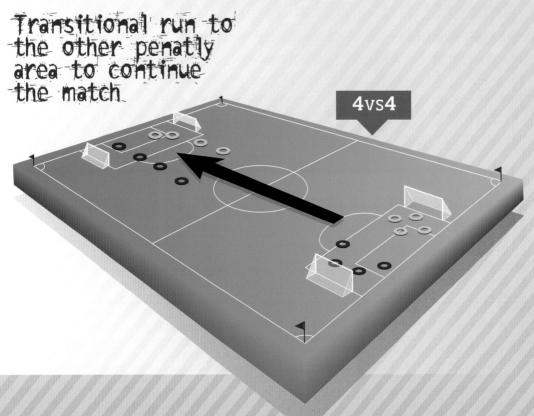

Transitional run to the other penalty area to continue the match

4vs4

Speed block

Here's an example of a speed drill that offers competition and football-specific functions. Rarely in football does a player hit peak accelerations or speed without having to co-ordinate themselves in relation to the ball, an opponent or a team-mate. In this drill, on the whistle, the offensive player has to race to push the ball around a mannequin and score in a small goal before his opponent can get around the goal to block his effort.

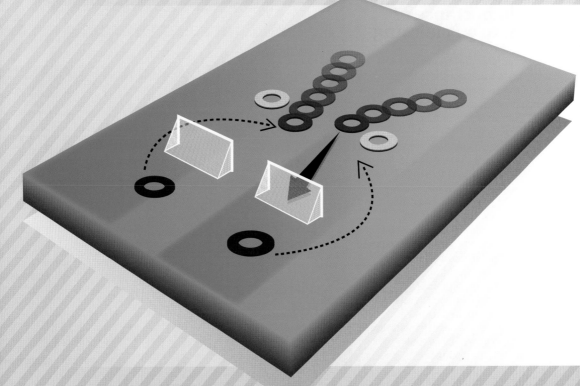

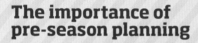

The importance of pre-season planning

The planning of pre-season actually starts up to three months before the end of the previous season. This is normally when the friendly matches need to be arranged, or tour schedules briefed.

Off-season programmes are given out at the end of the season and players are set targets for when they return so they can prepare for the demands of pre-season. The content and loading for the whole of pre-season is pre-planned and designed to give the players the base they need to help them stay fit and injury free throughout the season.

Variety and competition is so important to achieve good intensities and compliance in training but it requires time and thought in planning from the coaching staff so that standards can be maintained.

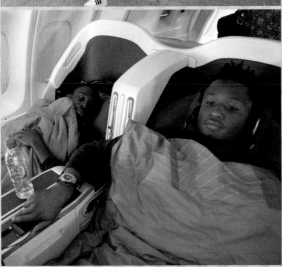

How do things change during the course of a season?

Once the season starts, it's all about making sure the players are sharp and ready for each game, as well as being fully recovered after each match.

The best and worst fitness regimes at this level may affect match performance by 5-10 per cent, but the difference pre-match readiness makes to performance can be over 30 per cent.

Basically, you can be very fit, but by doing too much, or doing the wrong things leading up to the game, the short-time energy stores are depleted and this will result in a lethargic display.

The teams that get this right the most have the best chance of achieving success. When the games start coming in thick and fast – during Champions League periods we also have to contend with late flights - recovering the players fully can be difficult. Individual assessments from our neuro-physiologists, Bruno Demichelis and Tim Harkness, can help determine players' fatigue levels.

Examples of the impact good fitness has made during a game

While we can't disclose confidential data collected from our testing, if we could clone a player with the aerobic capacity of Lampard, the strength of Drogba, the power of Essien, the agility of Ashley Cole, the speed of Anelka, the resilience of Malouda and the speed endurance of Kalou, we would have an amazing physical specimen on our hands.

It's usually the glamorous part of the game that gets linked with the impact good fitness has made in matches, such as scoring late goals. But, even though we've had a good record in these areas previously, it's other elements that I appreciate more – tracking back to defend after one of our own attacks breaks down, like Lampard or Malouda, an unselfish over-lap run that creates space for a team-mate, like Ashley Cole or Zhirkov, or the physical presence and brave defending of set-plays that Terry and Alex offer. This is the 'dirty work' that sometimes goes unnoticed and a lot of it is down to fitness.

Relationship with the coaches and manager

I've been fortunate to work with a number of managers as a fitness coach and physiotherapist at Chelsea over the past eight years, which has been a fantastic experience. It is important to have a close working relationship and the integration of the training ground staff at Cobham, from the top to the bottom, is extremely efficient and fluid. There are many people who should take a lot of pride from this, but it all starts, of course, with Carlo.

EAT LIKE
CHELSEA FC

A healthy diet is vital if you want to stay on top of your game. Making sure you have enough of the right stuff, and avoid foods which can be counter-productive, is the outlook of Nick Broad, Chelsea's Head of Sports Science...

Overall philosophy towards food

We have a Chelsea way of eating that, if adopted, will supply all the nutrients necessary for the players' training, wellbeing and competitive load. To do that, we recommend the players choose meals with an equal proportion of three different food groups, which from a scientific perspective are carbohydrates, proteins and vitamins, minerals and fibres.

We would re-label those groups so the players can engage with them more, calling them energy, protection and repair foods.

In our system, repair foods are equivalent to proteins, energy foods are carbohydrates and protection foods are fruits and vegetables, which provide the vitamins, minerals and fibre.

On top of that, players must have a healthy fat source attached to their diet. Healthy fat sources might be extra virgin olive oil, fat in seafood, nuts and seeds, olives, avocado and most importantly, the fat obtained from organic meats.

So, the strategy is this: one third of the plate for any meal should be protection foods, one third energy foods and one third repair foods and there should be a healthy fat source within that meal.

Examples of food groups

Within the group of energy foods (carbohydrates), we tend to talk about brown grains versus white grains. We want to drive more B vitamins into the players' bodies, and these are more prevalent in brown grain than in white grain.

As for repair food groups (proteins), we want meat that is 'lean and clean', meaning free-range organic meat and trimmed of any visible fat.

Within the group of protection foods (vegetables, minerals and fibre) we look for seasonal and locally grown produce, so our vegetables come from a farm 12 miles away and the players eat them less than 24 hours after they've been picked out of the ground. That means they contain more nutrients than if they've been flown from far corners of the world.

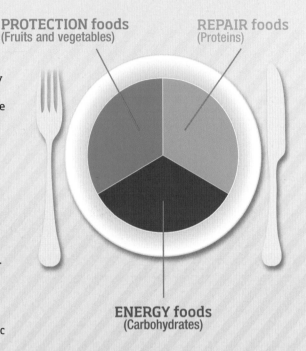

PROTECTION foods
(Fruits and vegetables)

REPAIR foods
(Proteins)

ENERGY foods
(Carbohydrates)

THE PERFECT MEAL:

REPAIR - Chicken or Salmon
ENERGY - Potatoes
PROTECTION - Vegetables

Energy foods (carbohydrates)	Repair foods (proteins)	Protection foods (fruit & vegetables)
Wholegrains Pasta Rice Bread Couscous Quinoa **Roots** Parsnip Turnip Potato Sweet potato Swede **Legumes** Beans Lentils Peas	**Lean meats** Game Poultry Fish Shellfish Beef Lamb Pork **Dairy** Cheese Yoghurt Milk **Eggs** Poached Scrambled Omelette Boiled	**Fruit** All - eat a variety of colours **Vegetables** All - eat a variety of colours **Legumes** Peas Beans Lentils **Nuts** All - except peanuts

Specialised supplementary drinks

What we recommend the players do on a day-to-day basis is no different to what we'd recommend to the public or to our youngsters in the Academy. This is why we set up the Chelsea way, so that a young player could follow it as well as a senior player.

Where the difference lies between professional sports and a member of the public, is that we are able to manipulate the recovery element to an extent by providing each player with a drink that is designed specifically to maximise their recovery from each training session and which is adapted to their workload that day.

In doing that, we are supplementing the carbohydrates, proteins and fats in the nutrition they take on board around training. Added to the eating philosophy that anyone can follow, it's this that separates the intake of a professional sportsperson from Joe Public.

Applying the Chelsea approach to your everyday life

Breakfast

Two poached eggs served on walnut bread, some berries and green tea

Here, the repair foods come from the egg whites, the energy foods from the bread, the protection nutrients are in the berries and there are some more nutrients in the green tea. The plate is made up of one third of each vital food group and you can also identify a healthy fat source in the walnuts from the bread and the egg yokes.

For a younger player, perhaps we might choose something more appealing to somebody of that age, like a bowl of cereal. But we would make sure that cereal was a high quality brown grain, then organic milk would provide some protein and, rather than a green tea, we'd go with freshly squeezed juice or a glass of water supplemented by some fruit.

Lunch

Wholemeal pasta and seabass with broccoli, carrots and sweetcorn

Here, the pasta is your energy source, the piece of seabass represents the repair food group and broccoli, carrots and sweetcorn make up your protection foods. Then you would plan your dinner to contain a different grain, a different protein source and some different coloured vegetables or fruits.

Evening meal

Meatballs in a tomato sauce on brown rice with a side salad

Brown rice is a different grain to your lunchtime energy food, meatballs in a tomato sauce provide the repair foods and you could then go with a salad for your protection food, picking different coloured vegetables, like tomatoes, beetroot or garlic. Then you could have berries for dessert - blueberries and blackberries, so you have all the colours represented across two meals.

Lunch and evening meals (post training)

Lunch and evening meals run on the same principle but you'd look to avoid doubling up on any foods. Again, one third of the plate must be repair foods, so fish, white meat, red meat - it doesn't matter as long as the quality of meat is high and it's lean and clean. Then a third energy foods, like wholemeal pasta, brown rice, wild rice, new potatoes or mash potatoes - but not fried potatoes.

Then at least three vegetables of three different colours because we believe different coloured vegetables provide different nutrients. We believe a player should take on board nine fruit and veg every day - three pieces of fruit and six different vegetables and, within that, we'd want five colours represented.

Our outlook on fat

We have no problem with fat, per se, at this club and we also don't think fat is the reason why people are unhealthy – if a football player is overweight, we believe it is down to over-consumption of carbohydrates or taking on board the wrong kind of carbohydrates.

We use whole milk dairy produce at Chelsea, because we think the fat and the protein in dairy work together and don't function in the same way without one another. Our spreads are butter, we have no margarine here because of the type of fat it is and the implications it has on human health, and we avoid low-fat yoghurts as well.

We divide fats into 'functional fats', which are healthy, and 'storage fats', which are unhealthy. Certain fats have jobs to do within the body and we try to encourage consumption of those – it's very difficult to gain weight from these because you eat them and then they go and do their jobs in the body. But there are other types of fat, that don't have jobs and they are stored as fat – we try to discourage the consumption of these.

There is also a distinction to be drawn between inflammatory fats and anti-inflammatory fats. At the moment people consume too much omega 6, which is in vegetable fats, margarines and meat from animals fed in the wrong way – this is an inflammatory fat. The fat stored in fish, for example, is anti-inflammatory fat, as is the fat found in animals reared on grass.

What do we avoid?

Our composition of plates into one third of each major food group certainly helps to direct people and that is our main philosophy. We do, however, have major concerns about drinks and snacks.

Drinks aren't recognised by the brain in the same way that food is, so it's very easy to consume excess calories and carbohydrates in drinks through over-consumption of fruit juice, soft drinks and even sports drinks in the wrong environment, can lead to problems. So we try to keep them to a minimum and, similarly, excess carbohydrates and fat can be consumed in snacks.

Typically, you'll see people snack on biscuits or chocolate and soft drinks and for me that's the worst combination possible – an excess of carbohydrates, with storage fats. Biscuits, long-life storage foods and a lot of ready-made meals will all contain inflammatory fats in the form of vegetable fat.

Limit excess carbohydrates and fats particularly in snacks

Good snacks

We would recommend snacks that provide players with nutrients from the three food groups as well as healthy, anti-inflammatory fats. So, for example, yoghurt with fruit, parma ham with melon, biltong or almonds with dried cherries. Within those four snack ideas you have a range of choices.

Then you can make existing snacks healthier, such as sandwiches. If a player came to me saying he likes to eat cheese and ham sandwiches within two slices of white bread, I would suggest one slice of good quality, wholegrain bread, in an open sandwich with prawns, avocado and salad on top. All of a sudden I've got energy foods in the wholegrain, protection foods in the salad and avocado and repair foods in the prawns.

Pre-match

This is a pretty boring meal in truth. We have to make sure the liver is full with carbohydrates because it's the liver that supplies the brain and a player needs to be mentally prepared before a game.

So we offer basic stuff – pasta, potatoes or rice with lean meats that will empty from their stomach as quickly as possible. We avoid fat in pre-match meals because it can slow down the rate at which food empties from the stomach – we'd sooner go for fish or a lean chicken breast. That way they get some energy foods, some repair foods and, although we don't push vegetables on matchday, we do offer them to the players – they can be pretty fibrous and this can sometimes upset the gastro-intestinal system if someone was approaching a big game for the first time, for example.

After that, there will usually be yoghurts and fruit available, but all fairly light stuff in general.

PLAY *LIKE*
CHELSEA FC

Now you've learned what goes on behind the scenes and the effort that goes into preparing yourself for matchdays, it's time to look at putting that into action on the big stage and discover what you can do to make it to the top. So let's ask the players themselves...

SCORE *LIKE*

DROGBA

Chelsea's number 11 has proved a prolific goalscorer over the years, but it takes a lot more than just good finishing to be considered a top striker. Here's where you can learn from the best...

DIDIER SAYS..
Lone striker

When you play alone, you need a special preparation, a special warm-up so that mentally you are ready, otherwise you cannot play right.

I think about what I am going to do to escape my marker, what I am going to do to score goals. I actually think about the way I am going to score my goal - I close my eyes and try to imagine it and sometimes it doesn't happen. But most of the time when you get it in your head that you are going to score a certain kind of goal, it happens. It's funny but you create something in your head, a desire to score, an attitude and everything can go like this in the game.

It's different with two up front, a completely different approach - you have to think with your partner, have the same ideas as him and not think only for yourself.

A forward's relationship with midfield

I think it's half instinctive and half your comprehension of how the game is going and your relationship with the midfielders behind. They have to give you the right ball because if your body is not open and they play a ball in behind, you can't score. So they have to look and see where you're going, put the ball in the right place for you to score without turning or changing direction.

The most important thing is to adapt your game to the opponent

Getting the better of your marker

I have to look at the defender's game but also I have to concentrate on my game and the way I'm going to receive the ball to score the goals. I think the most important thing is that you adapt your game to the opponent.

This is the fight of the game, a mental thing. At one moment you can know whether you have won the battle or lost it and from that you can win or lose the game.

Normally, you shouldn't think about this, you should be strong enough to just concentrate on yourself. But you also need to look at the defender – how is he breathing? If after one or two runs he is struggling, you say to yourself, "Okay, I'm going to do more runs to kill him." Or if you see that the guy is really confident, you know it's going to be difficult and then you have to change your game and try to beat him with the help of another player on your team.

If you are struggling one against one, then use somebody else in the move to beat that man. There are some games when you think to yourself, "Today it's going to be difficult to score, really difficult." So we think about that as well – you have to remember that as a striker you have plenty of time to change the physiognomy of the game.

Mixing up your playing style

As a striker, sometimes you are asked to play in different styles. In one system or a particular game, you might be dropping in to connect midfield and attack, but in another it might be all about anticipating what your team-mates and wingers will do, so you have to be meeting crosses and attacking balls in the penalty area.

I think I can play both ways just as well but it's true that I love to receive the ball into feet to be given the chance to try and create something, to pass to my team-mates and I think it makes me more unpredictable than in the other way because I can use my balance and my strength to help.

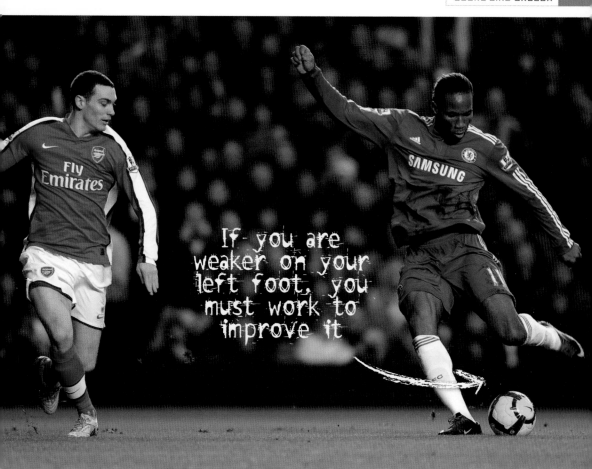

If you are weaker on your left foot, you must work to improve it

Improving your weaker foot

You have to try to improve both your feet if you want to play your best football. If you are weaker on your left foot, you have to do everything to improve it. If I find a weakness in my game, I will work on it because you need to put all your chances away to win games.

I was quite good with my left foot from a young age because I worked on it very hard when I was younger. Because of Maradona, I wanted to be left-footed! It's impossible but I tried and I worked on it so I could give passes with my left foot and shoot with it like him.

The art of scoring from free-kicks

I think I got my technique sorted last season – I scored some free-kicks two or three years ago but now my technique has improved so I'm more confident when I put the ball down and try to shoot.

It goes with pace but I shoot with my leg open with my side-foot. It's the place where you hit the ball that will give it the power, it doesn't come from the force of your leg, but the impact on the ball.

The way you control your leg gives a different speed or trajectory to the ball so that's what I practice and I practice a lot. A few other players do this, Juninho did it at Lyon and Juliano Belletti can do it as well. It makes it difficult for the goalkeeper because if the ball goes past the wall, it is going downwards and curling quickly.

SCORE *LIKE*
ANELKA

Goals win games, so if you want to become a proven match-winner, you need a predatory instinct and cool finish, but sometimes you have to think outside the box, just like Chelsea's versatile French forward...

NICOLAS SAYS...

The art of good finishing

When you have a chance to score, don't ask yourself any questions, have no questions in your mind as you face the goalkeeper. If you choose to do something, do it straight away because if you think too much about what you are going to do when you are one-on-one, you will miss. I make a choice in my head and go for it and that's why I've been able to score many goals in these situations. The ball comes and I finish.

If the keeper goes to ground, a chip over him can be a good option

SKILL TIP...

CHIPPING THE KEEPER: Sometimes the keeper will go to ground early and when you see him do this, you can try to chip the ball over him or place it to the side of him. To chip the ball you need to practise stabbing your foot under the ball to lift it slightly and get it back down so it doesn't drift over the bar.

Holding the ball up

Dropping deep

Through-balls

Running with the ball

Playing as a support striker

I've always liked to play as a number 9-and-a-half alongside someone else up front. I think of it as being like a striker but also in the middle of the midfield and attack. So I'm a striker but not at the top of the team and I'm still in the centre of the pitch – a bit like the position Dennis Bergkamp used to play.

He used to play for Arsenal like that when I was there, not like a striker but not a number 10 or a midfield player either, you play between the number 10 position and the centre-forward position, that's a 9-and-a-half.

My game is not to stay in the box – I don't like to wait in the box because I know I can do more than that. That's why I move where I can see space and look for other players in good positions to score sometimes. Also, I know that if I do this for my team-mates, then sometime in this game, or the next game, they will do it for me as well.

When you play at Chelsea, the most important thing is to win games as a team. If you play striker and you want to stay up front all the time, you won't touch the ball much and it's very difficult to enjoy the game. So, because I like to touch the ball and participate in the game, I have to come back sometimes and get a feel of the ball. In this team everybody can score, so even if I drop deep and come to the ball, someone can go beyond me and still use the space to score, which is good for the team.

Give and go   Start your run

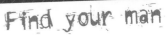

Find your man

Read the game and anticipate

I think in the position I play you need to know before you get the ball where your team-mates are and try to be clever because in modern football, doing something clever is advantageous. I try to learn what my options are before the ball comes to me and that's why sometimes you see me accelerate away, other times I come back and wait or other times I pass to a team-mate.

You have to be clever now, it's not enough just to be a very good footballer or very athletic because if you do not have the intelligence to make the right decisions on the pitch, I don't think you will make it at the highest level.

You have to try to analyse the play during the game and see where there is space. So sometimes you notice something early and then it can be really easy to make chances, but sometimes it is really hard to find space – then you have to keep looking and thinking because every game is different.

Look for the return ball

Shout to your team-mate

Getting the better of your marker

I think you always have to make it so that your opponent has to run after you and to mark you, not the other way around - so if the ball is loose, you must work hard to get there first. That makes it difficult for him, when he is always trying to stop you and not playing himself. But even when someone is getting close to you and marking physically, I think if you have something in mind, you have to try to do it anyway, don't let him stop you.

I also try to stay very calm always, so my opponents don't try to get in my head. It's the same that I don't kick people and so they don't kick me – sometimes when you respect the defenders, I think they respect you as well.

You can't score them all

Sometimes you miss good chances because you haven't scored one for four or five games, so the most important thing is to stay concentrated because you know when you play as a striker, maybe you will have just one chance and you need to do your best to score it.

If you miss, you have to stay patient and just try to do better the next time. I've had a lot of things happen in my life - a lot of clubs and a lot of situations where I've been up and down. So I know what to do when things don't go well and I've learned that the most important thing to do is be patient. Every time I have a bad period, I say to myself if I have chance to score, I will try my best and if I score, it's good; if I miss, that's life - I take it like that.

Patience is a virtue

I think you get more patience with experience but it is a very important part of being a striker, you also have to read the game well. Sometimes you have to calm the game down because there is no solution to pass the ball to anyone quickly.

So in this position, your game is to be patient, especially when you play against a smaller team and they stay back. If the team is in a rush, you won't have any chances anyway at the highest level - you have to be patient, it's part of the game. Then, if you score one goal, you maybe get the chance to score more because the other team has to come out and make the space for you to create more.

OWN THE WINGS *LIKE*
MALOUDA

Speed, control, vision, technical ability, delivery – just some of the attributes which can help you become a world-class winger like Florent Malouda...

FLORENT SAYS...

You don't have to beat your man to get a cross in

Sometimes, when you are a winger, you don't have much space or time, and to get a cross in you have to curl the ball around your marker. The first time I saw this it was the Brazilian national team and they love to do this, to curve their crosses.

Also I remember Ricardo Quaresma, when he was on loan here, could do it with the outside of his boot to change the direction of the cross.

I think it's a good way to make the cross into a dangerous area, even when you don't have a chance to run through into space.

Making the decision whether to run, to cross or to make a short pass depends on the runs of your strikers. Sometimes the striker doesn't have much time and space.

When I receive the ball and the striker is already in front of the defender or is going to get in front of the defender, I make a choice to give it straight to him. Sometimes the defender is close to me so I have no choice but to curl the ball around him and into the path of the striker.

Read between the lines

If you want to make space, you need to have clever movement off the ball, between the line of the other team's defence and midfield. Nowadays, with the tactical discipline of any team, it's all about trying to make time. You have to run around the back of the defender to turn him the wrong way and then you can start making your move. You have to make the space before you receive the ball, or you and the defender will arrive to it at the same time – you make the difference off the ball.

First you have to run outside the defender or defensive midfielder to turn him and then you have to change direction to lose him – it's all about changing direction at the right time. You need good co-ordination and good understanding with your team-mates for this because if you go left and he puts the ball to the right, you lose possession.

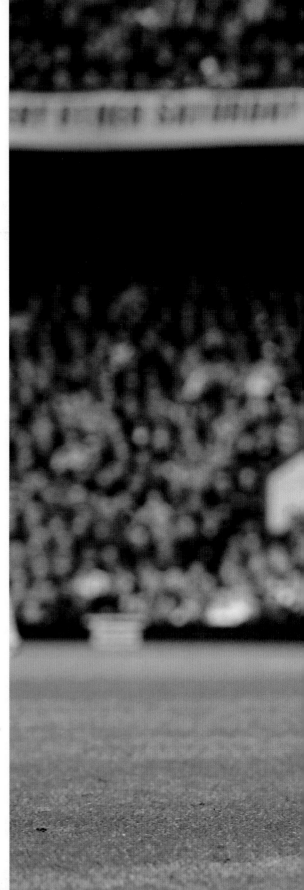

At Chelsea you have to move the ball quickly

Modern football is all about transition, both from defence to attack and between attackers. When you get the ball back from the opposition, you have to counter-attack very quickly, especially when the other team has come to defend in numbers when you are at home.

When you first win the ball back, that's the moment where you can make big differences, so you have to be quick, don't take too many touches or you're losing time.

Pick the right time to take your opponent on and beat him

I always look to see if there is cover behind him. If I'm one against one I have to try to go straight past him in the goal's direction - that's not a risk, it's part of your role, to make a difference to the shape of the pitch. But if there is cover, I try to analyse if I can draw them both close to me and then pass the ball to my team-mates so we can get more space between us.

I try to get the ball early and with my first touch go in the defender's direction, go past him and eliminate him from their defence. But if we have lost time in the transition between defence and attack, I have to wait for support so we can make a collective move.

Deep crosses and crossing from the byline

When you make an early cross from deeper, you have to put more speed on the ball into the box. The striker will be trying to make a run into the area and usually they want to score with one touch. So a strong, quick cross will be perfect if they want to touch or flick the ball past the goalkeeper.

But when I cross from the goal-line, I try to put a soft ball, a slight touch, because my team-mates will be behind me and need time to arrive onto the ball. The defender will try to run back quickly and if I put a sly ball over the top of the rushing defender, my team-mate has time to arrive as the ball lands for him. You can be more particular in your aim with a cross from the goal-line in who you aim for, rather than just putting it in the right area with speed like you do from deep.

Putting pace on a deep cross into the box can allow the striker to score with one touch

Placing a
ball with less
power from the
touchline gives
the striker time
and troubles
defenders

Look up and pick a
man out before you
cross

SKILL TIP...

DIFFERENT CROSSES: There are different ways of crossing a ball after you have beaten your man.

Powerfully driven low crosses into your opponents' penalty area – particularly on the edge of the six yard box – are notoriously hard to defend.

Such a cross creates uncertainty between the goalkeeper and his defenders as to who should take responsibility and there's always a chance of a lucky deflection going into the net.

If a winger has a big striker to aim for, or an attacking midfielder who times his runs late, then a chipped cross to the centre of the penalty area or far post can be most effective.

Another option, particularly when in a deeper wide position, is to cross the ball early before even taking on the full-back.

In requires a good first touch to cushion the ball in front of you, before attempting to curl the ball around your marker, but so that it arcs away from the goal.

This gives a striker the chance to attack your cross and may even draw the goalkeeper off his line and into no-man's land.

SKILL TIP...

GET YOUR HEAD UP: Crossing the ball isn't just about aimlessly hitting it into the box, but picking out a team-mate.

As you can see from these pictures, Florent Malouda sometimes crosses with his head up.

Rather than look at the ball, he's looking for the team-mate he is aiming for and that technique allows him to cross with precision.

To cross the ball low, then you must lean over it, but to float the ball into the box, then it's a case of leaning back slightly to get some backlift. Getting the correct body shape and striking the ball at the right angle are important if the cross is to be accurate.

Lean back too much and you're in danger of over-hitting it, strike it hard without looking and the chances are that you'll simply hit the first man.

Practise getting to the byline and trying to pick out a mate while another friend tries to intercept it.

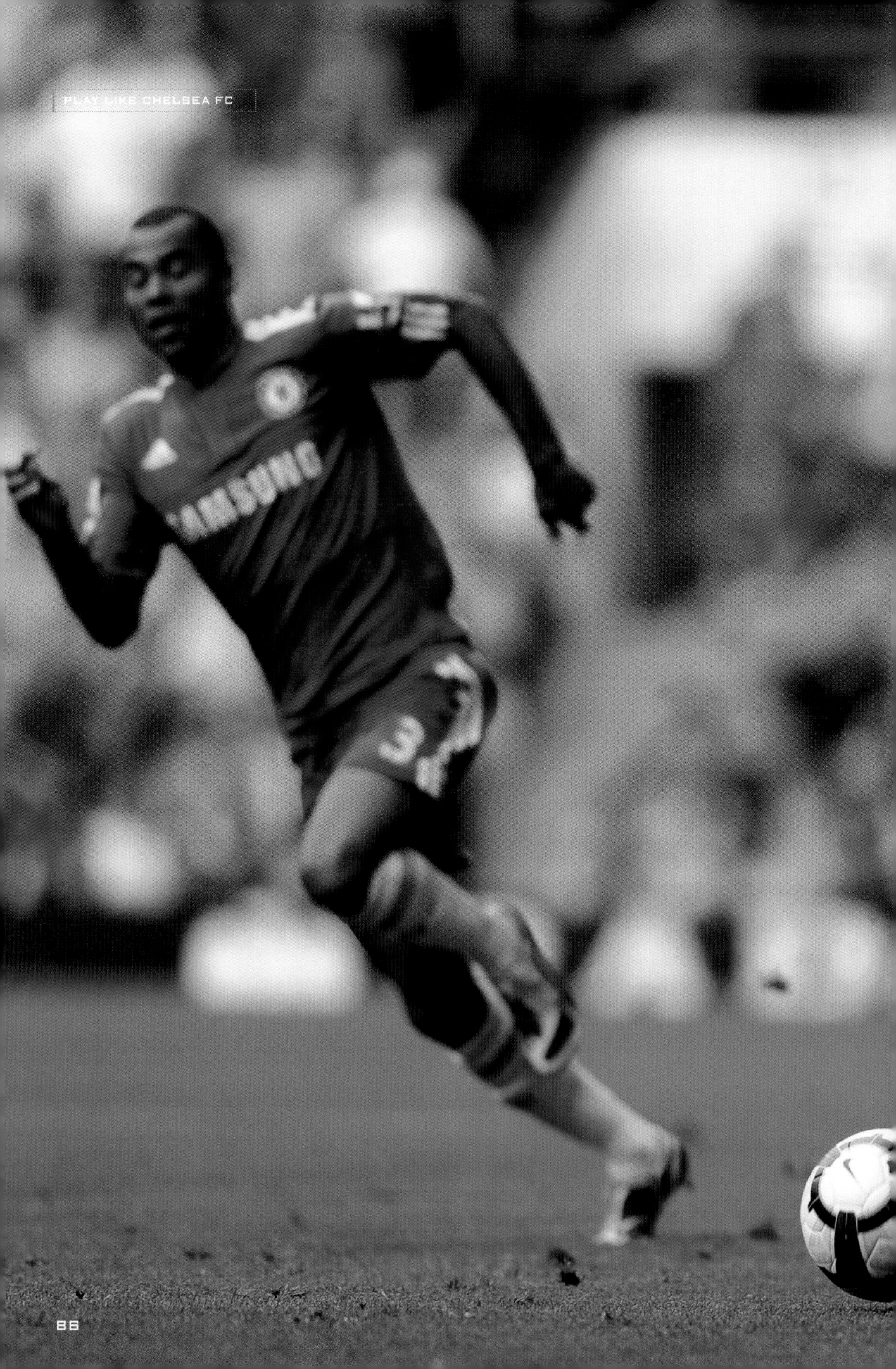
SAMSUNG

Have an understanding with your full-back

It helps me when Ashley comes forward to support me because he gives me a lot of space, the defender doesn't know if he has to come to pick me up or to follow Ash because he is always a problem for the defence. They don't know how to control a left-back who is always there to create problems for them.

So the good thing with the system we have and with all the midfielders we have, is that me and Ash can go forward, combine and create a lot of problems with our movement. We can come from far down the pitch together and there is always someone to overlap with us, so I can run really fast down the pitch and then someone gives me the ball behind the line of their defence, or he can do it and I drop deeper.

You need intelligence and communication between the players because sometimes you can see even Ash is always on the wing and we have to know how to keep the balance so that we can be free when we attack, but when we lose the ball, someone has to be covering because you have to secure your position.

Switching roles

The most important thing is not the system, it's the way you move within it and when a player tries to anticipate your move, you have to look at your partners and try to disturb the defence with movement.

That's why I sometimes try to come up on the right side and not just on the left, but the most important thing is that, once the action is finished, we come back to the main system to defend and then we can be free again when we attack.

You have to always be aware of the position of your partner for the replacement. That's the most important thing: that everybody knows what they have to do first and also that everybody knows the other players' role. We're trying to move and create space because we always meet teams who want to beat us and who make space tight for us.

I really enjoy having this freedom to move and create problems for the other teams and we feel on the pitch like they can't catch us because we're always on the move. That's the difference in us now and I believe it will help us to achieve the targets we've had from the beginning of the season.

ATTACK *LIKE*
KALOU
& BENAYOUN

Whether you're running at defenders, creating space with your movement, or making a key assist, it's important to provide support to your front line. As an attack-minded midfielder, or auxiliary forward, you can also benefit from a fair share of goals by following the model of Salomon Kalou and Yossi Benayoun...

SALOMON SAYS...

Attacking down the flanks

On the wing your aim is to stretch the game for the team and you are always at the beginning of the moves when the team starts to get on the ball.

Being a right-footed player, if I play on the left it means that I have to beat my man and deliver the right ball to my team-mates. It means I can also try to score myself by putting the ball on my right side in a good position to shoot.

Running at
defenders

Versatility and adaptability

At the start of the game I play behind the striker on the line-up, but the thing is Anelka and I can always switch positions. It doesn't matter who is in front or who drops back, there is always a good combination. I suppose it happens because he is the kind of player who likes to go to the ball and I like to run beyond the defence sometimes, so it gives us a choice of who plays behind.

I think I have played everywhere in midfield and attack under five managers since I joined Chelsea. I have to adapt to any situation because I am a professional and I am lucky that I can play many positions.

This season I am free to come inside and pick up the ball but I have to keep running at the opposition and put pressure on them - do the teamwork. After all, it's more about the team than one player and I have a job to do for the team.

Joining the front line

GETTING GOALS FROM WIDE POSITIONS: Scoring goals as well as creating them is an aspect of an attacking midfielder's game that must not be overlooked.

A successful team needs goals from every area of the pitch and those playing out wide have to make a contribution.

Salomon Kalou has weighed in with his fair share of goals and the fact he is a right-footed winger who often plays on the left has been a contributory factor as he will cut inside his man and attempt to curl the ball around the goalkeeper.

Shooting across the keeper is important as even if he manages to get a hand to the ball, he may only push it out to a team-mate who is lurking in front of goal.

A winger must also ensure that he gets himself into the box at the far post when the ball is on the other flank in an attacking area.

Doing so gives the man on the opposite wing an extra target to aim at and ensures there is someone in position to take advantage if a defender or goalkeeper goes for the cross and misses it.

Kalou was in the right place at the right time to get this goal against Stoke and indeed on a further two occasions during the match, claiming the match ball with a hat-trick in the 7-0 rout.

It's all about decision-making when you're a winger.

Confidence comes from being out there on the field

Strikers thrive on confidence. It's about playing, getting on the pitch every week so that they know how you want the ball, when you are going to get in front of the goal and when your team-mates know this they make more opportunities for you to score. Also, the more you play, the more you build up confidence, it doesn't just come to you fast, it's something that grows when you are on the pitch, doing it every week.

In football now you don't need a lot of years and matches to show what you can do. Some players who are still youngsters have the best seasons of their lives and then they become important players in football, not youngsters. Look at how well Messi and Ronaldo have done when they are still young.

It's all about being on the pitch, developing yourself every day and I learn a lot from being at Chelsea.

Giving it your all

I think the most important thing in Premier League football is keeping the fighting spirit in your team. You can't just play at 50 per cent because the other team will then come at you with 100 per cent and you'll get knocked out. You have to always be aware which can be difficult when you first move to England, but once you're used to it, you can keep your concentration.

I've had to work on my body strength here because it's about strength and power, not just technique.

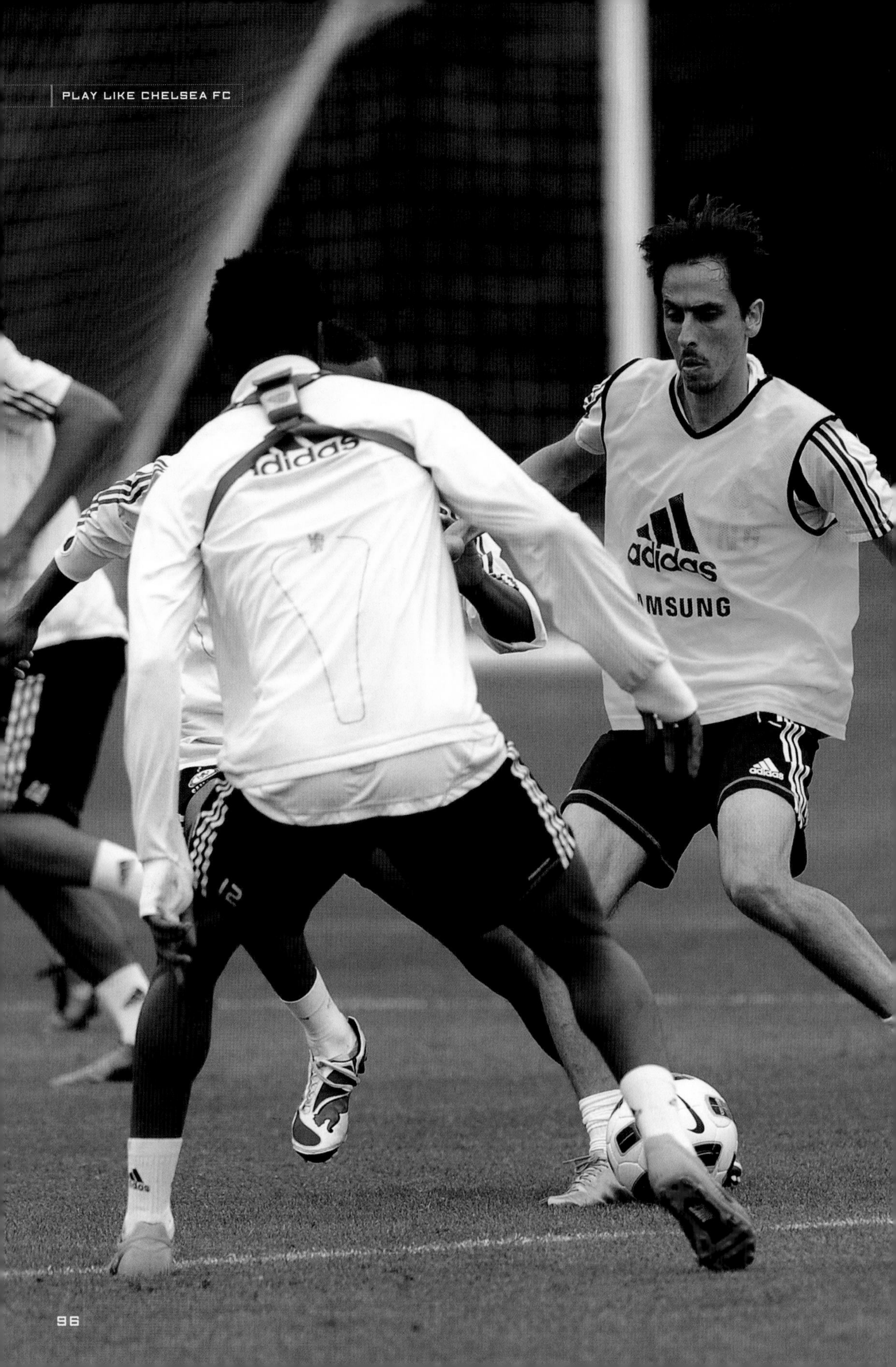
adidas
adidas
AMSUNG

SKILL TIP...

BETWEEN THE LINES: For attacking midfielders like Yossi Benayoun, playing 'between the lines' is an important discipline to master.

If your manager asks you to play between the lines then it means he wants you to operate in the area between the opposition's defence and midfield.

An attacking midfielder playing in that role can be particularly difficult to mark as often a centre-half will be attracted to him, breaking the defensive line.

By pulling a centre-back out of position it creates space for team-mates to run into, so anyone playing between the lines must be good on the ball, have quick feet in order to beat a defensive midfield marker, and show intelligent movement.

The ability to play first-time passes, particularly one-twos, is vital, while such players must also be able to play accurate through passes for strikers to latch on to as they will regularly find themselves in space in attacking areas.

A lot of those qualities are found in wingers so some managers will ask a wide player to play in a central position between the lines.

Benayoun is a fine example of a player who is not only comfortable playing in both roles, but also contributes goals.

PLAY *LIKE*
LAMPARD

Every successful team needs an inspirational figure. Someone capable of covering the whole pitch, scoring crucial goals and providing key assists. Frank Lampard has been that man at Chelsea for almost a decade. Here's how...

FRANK SAYS...

The midfield role

You have to be a team player and, as a midfielder, you have to see the potential passes from deep and also be able to get up there and be around the opposition box – that's what the best ones do. And as an all-round midfielder these days, you don't just have to pass and contribute, but you have to score goals.

If I can give a lot to the team in defensive terms and make more assists or score more goals than others who play behind the frontman, then I feel like I'm doing my job.

You also have a lot of other responsibilities as an all-round central midfielder, you need the energy to get up and down the pitch, defend and everything else. So I'm quite proud that my goal-scoring record puts me ahead of attacking midfielders if you like. I don't class myself as an attacking midfielder because there are a lot of players out there who play with a lot less responsibility than me in midfield.

It's important to pick out your pass early and not dwell on the ball

Learn from others and be aware!

It's very important to be open to learn and to watch. At every level of football, you can see instances in games where you think about what you would do differently.

I also think it's important to be aware of other players' runs and when to put them in on goal with a pass. I'm always looking instantly for that pass and playing with Didier Drogba and Nicolas Anelka you know they're always waiting for that ball in behind so there's no point in waiting around or wasting any time delivering it.

I watch football and I think sometimes people miss the early ball when there's a bit of space for someone else, so I always look to do that when I'm playing.

Movement off the ball

This is something I've learned and improved since I've been playing. I didn't move in the same way when I was a young boy at West Ham or when I first came here. I think I was running a lot more in straight lines and I was probably a bit one-dimensional in the way I was trying to arrive in the box.

But you learn from experience, from playing with good players who make good movements themselves and then you can make moves off of them – you learn something new from doing that. I think Drogba and Anelka are fantastic in the way they use pace and movement and I try to make

space from their movement. People are worried about them, especially when they're running in behind defenders and pushing the defensive line back because that opens up space and makes it easier for me to arrive in space when the ball comes into the box.

That's all due to their movement and I just need to make a run to arrive in time, so a lot of it, then, is about having the stamina to get up there. Also a lot of knowing where to run is based on learning from my team-mates and from my own experience, although I'm sure it takes some natural ability as well to see the spaces opening up.

The Chelsea way is to move the ball quickly

I'm a big believer in fast football, I hate possession for possession's sake. To keep the ball and play slowly is the most dangerous thing in football because you can let the other team nick the ball off of you and counter-attack. When we are playing well we keep possession, but we move it quickly and that's when teams can't live with you. The easiest way I ever score goals is when we win the ball back and move it quickly forward. What's the point in winning the ball back and just keeping it?

To chip the ball, get your foot under the ball and try to judge how much lift to put on it

SKILL TIP...

I've scored a few chips over the years and it is something I've tried in training many times. When I'm feeling more confident in my game, it's something I like to try because you can catch people unaware by doing something different every now and again.

I know people expect me to smash shots from outside the box, so sometimes you can catch the keeper unaware with a chip if you get your foot under the ball, lift it and weight it right. It's about trying it out in training to get the right amount of power and once you've got an idea and the confidence to try it in a match, it's obviously very satisfying to score that kind of goal.

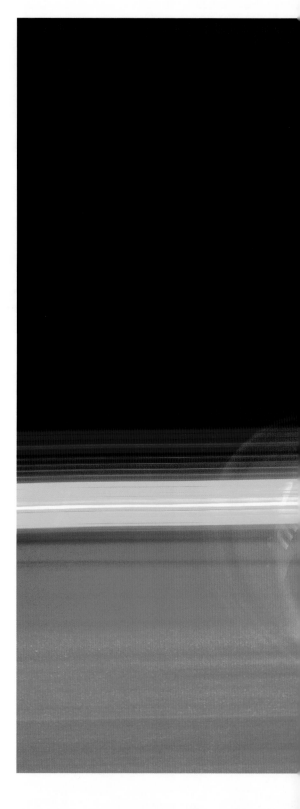

Work hard on your weaknesses but don't forget your strengths

At an early age, advice on my game would only have come from my dad and the best thing he taught, right from the moment I started playing competitively, was to work very hard and work on your weaknesses. To do that you need to spot your weaknesses very early and mine were probably my stamina and my athleticism at that age, I couldn't get around the pitch very well - so I worked very hard on that in my low teen years so I could get up and down the pitch through the games and that's obviously paid big benefits for me.

My dad saw the game changing, becoming faster, even when he was playing but more so when he'd finished. I think he saw a little bit of a lack of speed in me as a kid so he worked hard on my speed and all-round agility, which helped because it gave me a mentality to work on those things throughout my career. It also gave me a bit of extra sharpness at that time, which I think I've improved as I've got older.

So I've always done training on individual stuff after sessions to improve on weaknesses or maintain my strengths.

I find it's more important to get those extra bits of training in than it is to save myself at times, even if it does mean that I'll feel slightly tired some evenings in the week. I'd rather know I've been working on the things I need to work on, shooting with my left foot and extra running.

I've found that if you work on things a lot in training then you become lucky in games, balls fall to you and stuff like that. So if I run up and down a lot during the week and then arrive in the box to score in the 90th minute, I feel as though the practice has helped me to get that bit of luck. I suppose I think practice makes you lucky and I'll probably continue to do that extra training until I can't play anymore.

Try to add some new things to your game

I often work on new things and some of that comes from training, but some of it comes from experience as well. In some ways you feel more comfortable in yourself as you get older, I've certainly found that anyway.

I've had some really good years here and as I get older, every year I take a look at myself and at my game. I watch more games as well now and I see different openings and become aware of different things on the pitch.

There was a period when I started to score more headed goals and that was probably just to do with me working hard on my heading in training, but my improvement in things like arriving in the box at the right time is from looking at the game and working out a few things about when or where to arrive.

I like to try and bring something else to my game regularly, I think it's important and I get those new things for different reasons, whether it be practice, watching games or just learning from experience.

Consistency

It comes from doing things right. I don't think you can think about consistency and then achieve it. You do need an element of luck because injuries can break your season up and things like that can happen out of your control. But only by doing the right things, taking each week, each game and each busy period as it comes, can you be consistent.

You cannot perform consistently if you're not prepared. I don't care if you're Lionel Messi or any other player, if you're not training right, preparing right, resting right, you can't be consistent on the pitch. So all those things you do off the pitch and in training come into play during the game and they're the reason why I've been consistent I think.

If you don't put the work in, you won't get the goals, I don't have any issues with that and so I never get complacent. I'm aware that if I don't do the right things, I won't get the goals. I've not got a God-given talent to score 20 goals a season just by walking round a football pitch.

HOLD MIDFIELD *LIKE*

MIKEL
& RAMIRES

The modern game has a growing reliance on midfield enforcers and few are better at it than Mikel and Ramires. A combative and powerful presence between midfield and defence, they can dismantle any opposing threat, while their passing and awareness helps propel Chelsea forward...

MIKEL SAYS...

The holding midfield role

I love playing in the holding role, it's all in the head and you must be a quick thinker. You have to be a good passer of the ball as well because the team has to play around you.

When you play as a holding midfielder, you have to be extra focused, you have to be always behind the team, everything relies on you so you have to calculate and know what you are doing. It's about being where you need to be at the right time and the right moment - you have to have all those things in your head when you play this role.

If you don't do these things, it's not only you who doesn't play well, but the whole team - the team is not going to be compact unless you do your job properly.

I'm there to break up the attacks of the other team and to pick up the ball and start things. I have to drop in deep, pick up the ball and make sure we start playing from the back - put the right balance in the team and make sure we play how the manager wants us to play because this is what he asks me to do.

Sometimes you
get an urge to
go forward, but
you can't leave
your team-mates
vulnerable

Resisting the temptation to get forward

When you play in the holding role you have to cover for everyone, so there's always a lot of running, but I'm happy to do a lot of running, I've been happy to do that since I've been at Chelsea.

I do get an urge to go forward sometimes and I do want to get on the scoresheet, but you don't want to leave your position because that's like the engine room and when you leave it, the team is in trouble. So, yes, I want to get on the scoresheet but my position is more important and that has to come first, it's about self-discipline.

RAMIRES SAYS...

Brazilian influence

The centre of midfield and particularly the holding role is a very special position in Brazilian football and some of the most important players in the country's history have played there. I always liked to play in the middle when I first started playing football, even when some people said to me that it's a complicated position to try to make it as a footballer in because so many people want to play there. I always liked it and I think if you do well there, then you should keep playing, no matter how many other people want to play in the same position.

Be prepared

In midfield, you have to be ready all the time, whatever the situation is in the game. In this position, when your team is in possession, you have to be ready to receive the ball and, if the opposition is in possession, you have to be ready to help your team-mates defend.

That's why I chose to play in the middle, because my physical strength helps me to excel here - I work hard and I can run a lot and to play there you need these physical attributes. But it is not just hard work, you can make the play and sometimes you can get forward and attack as well, so I think it's important to enjoy it.

ATTITUDE

STRENGTH

VISION

MENTALITY

PLAY LIKE ESSIEN

Regarded as the engine room of the team, there are some skills every central midfielder needs in order to command the middle of the field...

You need to be strong on the ball

WHAT ATTRIBUTES DOES A CENTRE-MID NEED?

Energy, stamina and strength

First of all, you need a very good engine to be a midfield player. You need to have energy and stamina to be able to patrol the field and keep the team moving at all times. Similar to a marathon runner, you need to plan your game in such a way that when the opposition run out of steam, you will still be going strong. Making the necessary and important runs at the right time is crucial to this.

Secondly, you need to be strong if you want to boss the midfield. Strength is very important because you are able to hold onto the ball longer and no-one can push you off it. Your strength will ensure that you can take possession of the ball and keep it until you are ready to pass it on.

Vision and awareness

Every great midfielder needs vision. You should be able to have a mental picture of your team and opposition at all times to be able to pick the right pass. Without looking, you can pick a pass if your vision in midfield is right.

As well as having great vision, awareness is important because it helps a midfielder to always look for the next passing option before he receives the ball. If you spot one or two options before you receive a pass, you can always open up defences with a great pass or you at least keep the ball moving.

Having awareness helps you spot a pass early

Availability

Availability is always important in the middle of
the field. To keep a move going you always have to
be available to collect and pass and move the ball
on - available to defenders to start moves, available
to other midfielders when they are probing and
available to the strikers when they can't move
forward and need to offer a pass. It's very
important that you always try to be available.

Confidence

Confidence is another asset you require to play in midfield and in any position for that matter. Having confidence in your ability to receive and pass the ball, score goals and play well, is very important. Without confidence you will make mistakes and your game will not go as well as you want it.

Love of the game

Finally, to be able to show all these qualities, you have to love the game and enjoy it every time you step on to the pitch. You should always look forward to playing and giving it 100 per cent and if you can love the game and give it all you have, you will certainly do well.

BASIC SKILLS AND DRILLS

You also need to learn what I class as the basics to be able to be a complete midfielder...

Keep your eye on the ball at all times

Timing tackles

In midfield, one of your main jobs is to break up the opposition's play and timing your tackles are an important part of that. There is nothing wrong with a good fair tackle, but it is important to keep your eye on the ball at all times and win it fair and square. You need to feel you are within reaching distance of the ball and then go for it. The trick, as I have said, is to focus on the ball and go for it when you feel it's there for the taking.

There are times when you come up against a tricky player and you feel the chances to tackle them are limited. Fast players always drive at you and it's difficult to time your tackles when playing against them, so it's always best to tackle them when you are 100 per cent sure you will get the ball or just hold them up by staying on your feet and driving them on to their weaker side while you wait for your team-mates to support you.

Channelling your aggression

I think off the pitch I'm a quiet person, I don't really
like talking or doing interviews, but when I'm on the
pitch, that's a different thing altogether. The pitch is
like my office and when you're in the office, you don't
mess around - you mean business. So when I'm on the
pitch, everything switches and I go with my football
and do everything to try to win the game.

Passing and shooting

Both passing the ball and shooting are skills that need to be mastered when you are a central midfielder. In this position you keep the team ticking with your passing and you should always be around the opposition box to shoot any loose balls.

The key though, is all about decision-making, knowing when to pass and when to shoot. You pass the ball when the team have the momentum and are in possession. You need to look for a couple of passing options at all times to keep the shape of the team and to surprise the opposition. It's always good to mix your passes and as soon as you pass the ball, you either go for a return or get closer to relieve your team-mate in case they get pushed back or tackled.

On the other hand, shooting can come naturally and with instinct - some great shots are not planned. Also you can shoot when your team is tightly marked and there are no options. Rather than pass it back, you can shoot if you feel the opportunity is there. Always make sure you are within the frame of the goal posts and aim for the corners. Shooting has to be practised if you are to be really good at it.

When I strike the ball for a shot, I try to have something in mind and I try to hit the shot how I imagine it. Like the goal I scored against Barcelona in 2009 for Chelsea's goal of the season - as the ball was dropping, that was the only option I had in my mind, so I tried to hit it as I was imagining and I hit it well.

You know sometimes, when you hit the ball well, you get the feeling that the ball is going in, and I got that with this one. It depends how you take it, but if you hit the ball just right, you get the feeling in your boot that the ball is going where you want it.

How to stop the opposition

In midfield you are the cover for the defence, so you need to be on your guard to stop all attacks before the defence is put under pressure. Depending on what formation your coach decides to play, you may be asked to man-mark an opponent or be asked to operate within a certain zone.

As a defensive midfielder, your job will be to screen the back four and start all the moves for your team. You need to press the opposition high up the field when you don't have the ball so you can gain it back as soon as possible. But whichever position in midfield you are, you need to stay on top of your game and carry out every instruction given by your coach.

Press the opposition when they have the ball

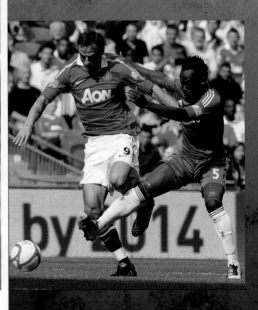

Train to maintain your skills

Practice makes perfect, so whichever position you play, you need to keep practising always. I train with my colleagues all the time (sometimes on Christmas day) so that I can stay sharp for games. I practise shooting, passing, positioning and work on my stamina all the time.

DEFEND *LIKE*
TERRY

English centre-halves are regarded as some of the most robust and commanding figures in football. Brave, committed and a reassuring influence on the whole team, none come more imposing than John Terry, a leader on and off the pitch...

JOHN SAYS...

Leadership on the pitch

Being a captain as a defender, I think it's easy for us at the back to be able to see things and get people into areas that we see are dangerous. By doing that, we can stop other teams getting through the middle of our team and force them wide, by which time the likes of Lamps and Essien can get back and we get our shape back. Then, having eight or nine players to break down rather than four or five defenders is obviously much better for us.

So, defensively, we try and force teams and players wide and hope that the midfielders use the time that gives us to recover our shape and we stay as a solid base.

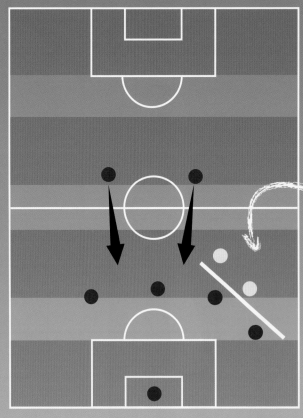

Forcing opponents wide allows time for your midfielders to drop back and help the team to regain its shape

Leadership off the pitch

You can never take a back seat, I would never do that anyway because it's something that's been instilled in me from a very young age and it's part of my job to get people around me going. If players are feeling tired or we have only got two days between matches, it's part of my job and other players' here to speak with everyone and make the most out of the time we have got so that we start all these games well and right.

Positive body language on the pitch

Always welcome new players and younger players to the group

It's brilliant to get new people involved with the squad and it's great for us to try help them through the situation that we've all been in. I had the help of Dennis Wise, Frank Leboeuf and Marcel Desailly, players like this, when I first started, so it's great for us older players to pass our knowledge on.

I remember Jimmy Floyd Hasselbaink's reaction to me when I was just coming into the team actually - we always had a few ding-dongs, me and Jimmy, but he was brilliant. He'd get the hump with me in training but afterwards he'd get me in a headlock and say: "That's brilliant, I love that, make sure you keep doing it!"

I'll do everything I can to stop us conceding a goal — even if that means taking a ball in the face!

Commitment

I'm living every boy's dream, I know that and I just want to make sure I give it everything and if that means taking a ball in the face or anywhere, I'll do it to stop a goal.

I'll do everything I can to stop us conceding a goal - I'm passionate about clean sheets, I hate it when we concede. I think that's just how passionate I am about it and I think I've got an understanding with the Chelsea fans and have done ever since I came through the ranks at this club.

For me, that comes from knowing what it means to them, and for us players, knowing that we can make the fans' weekends great and make their lives great because they love the football club and follow us all over the world. So we owe them everything every weekend and every time we pull on the shirt.

Anticipation

I think anticipation is one of those things people talk about that you're either born with or you don't have. From a very young age, even when I played in midfield as a kid, I read the game well. I've never been the quickest of players but thankfully I've read the direction of the game and read passes very well; my dad always used to say to me: "If you're half a yard or two yards ahead upstairs, then you don't need the pace to get there." I've not had the pace, that's not a choice I've made, but that anticipation is something you're born with.

Defenders can be technically good too

I've worked very hard all through my career, from the youth team days up to now, practising with my right and left foot. And I'm confident now that, on a longer range of passing, my left foot is as good as my right.

Central defensive partnership

Having a mobile, covering centre-back alongside a big centre-half who's willing to go and attack the ball, win the ball and throw themselves in front of everything, works really well.

If you're playing against a team with one up front, it just depends if the striker drifts into your defensive partner's area or your own area and if he has the ball and is coming towards goal or not. Normally I go forward and Alex drops off so if he does beat one of us, the other one's always going to be there covering. By that time, you'd expect your midfielders to get back and get alongside you to outnumber them.

In the middle, we don't often get caught one v one and that's the way we like it really - we force our opponents wide because we'd rather be one v one out there than in the middle.

Out wide, Ash knows he can show them inside or outside depending on the situation, it's not always best to show them the line. If he knows I'm inside him marking, I will tell him to show his man inside so we can double up. But if I've got a man with me, then I'll tell him to show his man outside and hope someone will track back and make a two v one situation out there instead.

Adapting to different strikers

I think you have to react differently to different players because there are the quick players, or players who like to come deep and link up well with the midfielders and bring other people into play. Then there are strikers who play on your shoulder and eight times out of 10 they're offside, but on those two occasions he isn't, he could race away from you.

So it's just knowing the different strikers - knowing what their assets are, what their weaknesses are and trying to get them into an area where they're forced into their weaknesses all the time.

You're never too big to learn

I'm always looking to learn and improve and when a manager comes in like Ancelotti, I think I can learn an awful lot from him - he's played and managed at the highest level himself. I've spoken to him a few times about Paolo Maldini as well and what he did, the way he worked, his relationship with the other players.

Every time I work with a different coach or manager I can always look at it as a chance to get my learning cap on and I can do that by talking to him about players that he's worked with as well.

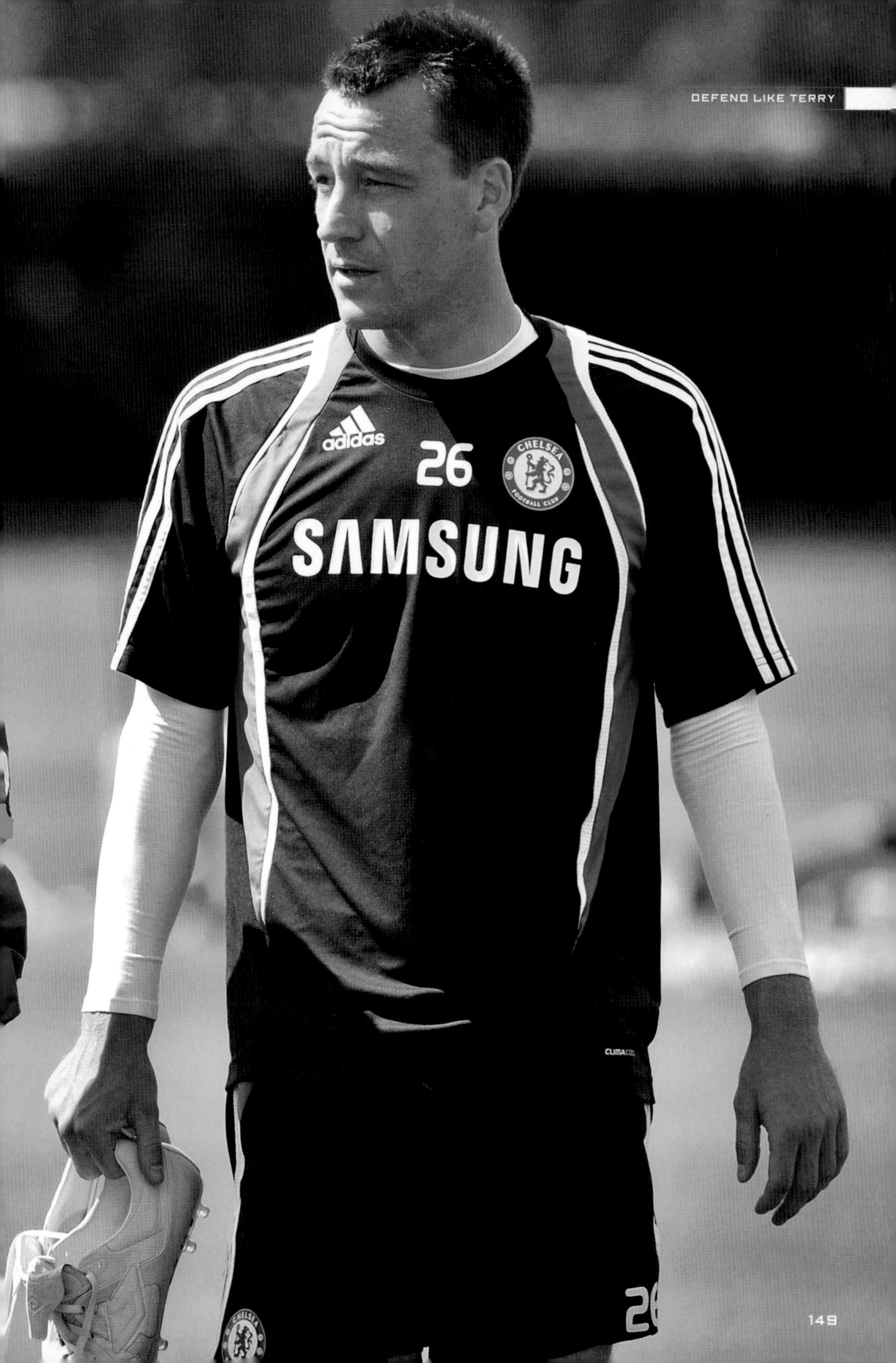
adidas
26
CHELSEA
FOOTBALL CLUB
SAMSUNG

BRING THE BALL OUT OF DEFENCE *LIKE*

ALEX

The first point of attack is the defence, so it helps to have a ball-carrying centre-half like Alex ready to inject some momentum and provide an attacking outlet...

ALEX SAYS...

Intercept and counter-attack

You have to think quickly and move quickly, you have to know when their man will give the pass. You have to be careful, pay attention to the ball and have confidence in your judgment that you will take the ball and only the ball. Then you must try to keep the ball so you can counter-attack quickly.

Supporting attacking moves

It's good to help the midfield, so it's important to make yourself free sometimes. If there is only one striker for the opponent, then you can look at your other defender so he knows what you are doing and go up to help your team-mates further forward. It is a surprise for the other team, so it can work well, but it's important that when one of the defenders is gone, someone else can cover him there, like Essien or Mikel.

It is very important for a defender to be able to run free into the space. It can often give the opponent's defence a lot of trouble, so I know it can be a useful thing for us.

It is very difficult for defenders if a centre-back from the opposition comes forward – I know this as a defender myself. So we know it makes life more difficult for us at the back, we try to do it ourselves. We try to do it at a time that will take the other team by surprise and that's why you can't make the runs all the time, only when you see the space. So I'm happy that I can put myself in a position to exchange passes with a midfield player or attacker and be in a position where I can score goals to help the team.

There is a little bit of instinct but I think this is the case with most players. When you see a space, each one of us can go forward because if a game is 0-0, especially at home, you want to try and change the game or improve the situation in any way you can. It depends how the game develops as to whether you make these decisions and I think these instincts have helped me to score a few goals in my career.

Scoring from set-pieces and loose balls

The most important thing is to have the right attitude, the instinct to attack. Myself, I always go up for set-pieces and try to head the ball, that's how I've scored most of my goals, as well as direct free-kicks, which are a speciality of mine. If you have the initiative to go forward and contribute, then hopefully it will work out for you.

Free-kicks

I have always hit the ball very hard and I developed this into a free-kick technique by training it. Nowadays the balls are changing and every time they develop, it makes life more difficult for the goalkeepers and easier for the guy taking the free-kicks. I find hitting the ball very strong makes it more difficult for the goalkeeper to save these new balls, but it was a natural talent - strength - that I have trained hard on in these situations.

Before the game, we talk about free-kicks, so when they are closer to the goal, the other players take them - either Lampard or Drogba. But when they are from long distance, which is my speciality, I take them. We make arrangements before and at half-time, depending on how the game develops, and decide who will take them. The other players take free-kicks on a line-up, someone takes the first one, then someone else and so on, but I take them if the ball is further from goal.

Communication is the most important thing

Defensive partnerships

Communication is the most important thing in a defensive partnership. Whether I play with John Terry or Branislav Ivanovic, what's important is the communication between us. We have to pay attention to the man we are marking and to each other. We also have to keep the same aims, for us the motto is 'no goals' – me and Petr say this to each other before each game, 'no goals', so it's a simple mentality but we have to be strong and pay attention.

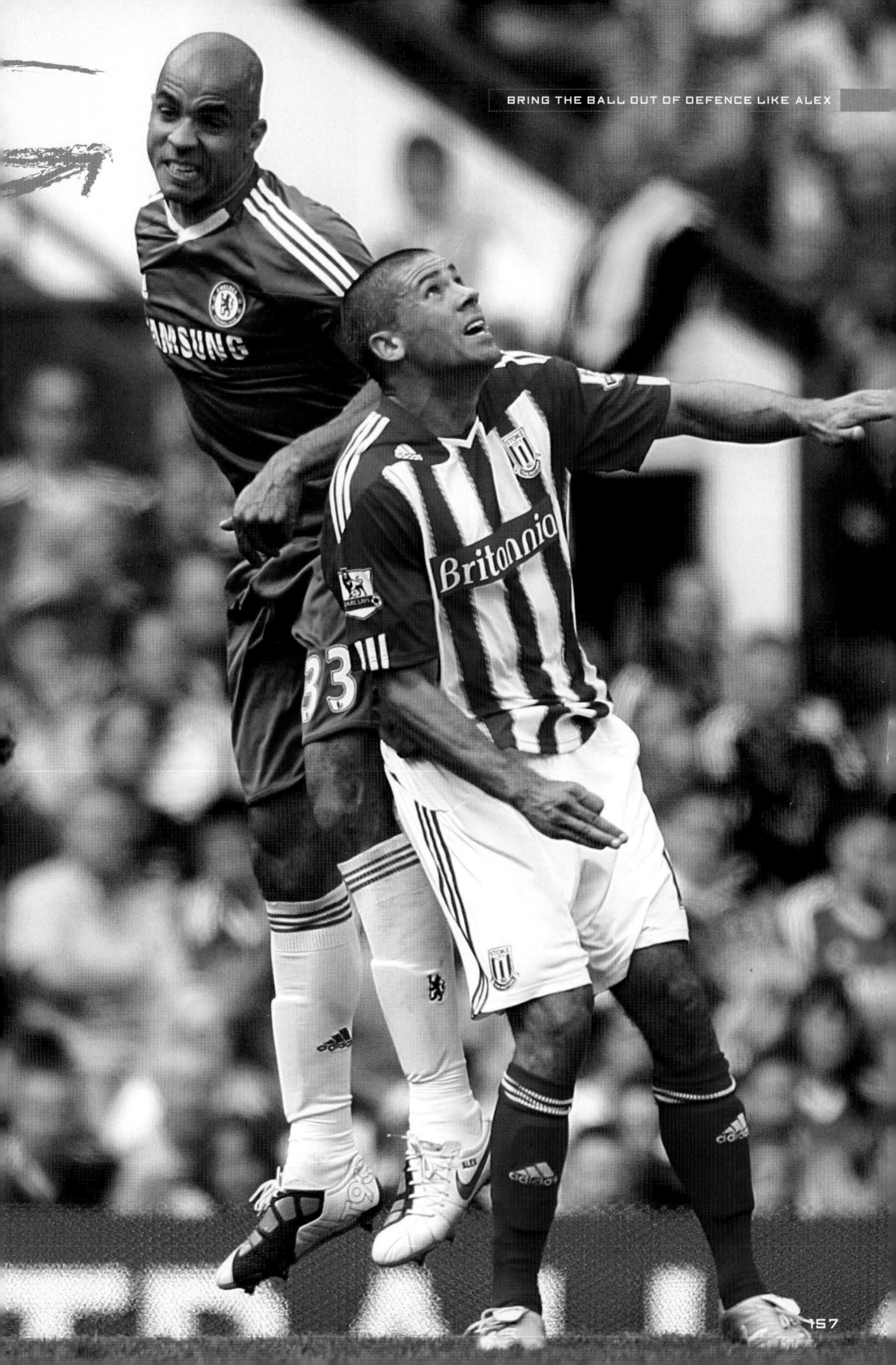
SAMSUNG
Britannia
33

Dealing with lone strikers or two up front

It is much easier to mark one man between two defenders because then you can play with one defender going up and down the pitch, running against their midfielders and putting them under pressure. Of course, you have your own midfielders to help you, especially at Chelsea where the midfield is so strong.

There is always a spare man when you mark one striker, but against two it is harder because you always have to be focused on your own man.

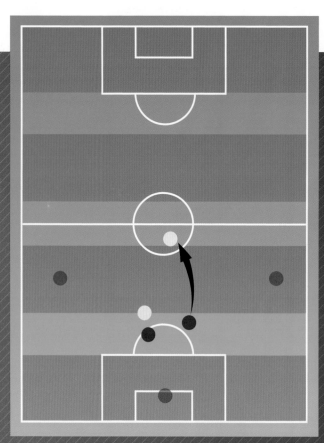

Two on one - one stays back, the other goes forward

Cultural differences

In Brazil, you have more chance to attack as a defender and make mistakes, but here if you make mistakes, it's a goal. So you have to play very quick and realise that the opponent will counter-attack if you make a mistake. In England, you don't have time to get back and defend if you are in the wrong position, so you must be very careful.

ATTACK FROM THE BACK *LIKE*
CHELSEA FC

Full-backs play one of the most active roles on the field as they shift focus from defence to attack, but you have to know when to venture upfield and when to be more cautious...

ASHLEY SAYS...

When I first started playing left-back, there were things missing from my game - you can't always be perfect. So there were things for me to learn and I think I always will learn, but it definitely helped coming through at a big club from such a young age with players like Tony Adams, Martin Keown and Sol Campbell, who had been around the game a long time.

I learned a lot from them and they said being a great defender is about positioning and, at that time, mine was all wrong - they said I attacked at the wrong times and although it worked at times, I was sometimes in the wrong places when I attacked. They were always giving me advice about when to go, what side of the player to mark and things like that.

That was how I started to learn the position and these days I've been there for years, so I know how important it is to defend as a unit.

Sometimes people say I've done well against a particular winger, but it's not just about me marking one guy - I think the players around me always help out, so when I show someone inside, they're there to take the ball off them.

When you play against top sides, it's not about stopping one player, so it's not just about me marking Messi or Walcott or someone like that, it's about the team. If we all play well, it makes everyone's job easier.

It's important to attack as a pair with the wide man on your side, so I work with Florent Malouda a lot. The way I look at it, if I do that, they've got to mark me as well because if they don't, then it's me and Flo against their right-back.

You need to have the fitness and energy to get up the pitch and back again, but there are lots of lazy wingers out there who don't want to track back too much and I try to take advantage of that as much as I can.

BRANISLAV SAYS...

I have a role to play where there is quite a lot of one-on-one action. This is the way it works in English football because players take each other on individually through the game. In these situations it's important that you are better than your opponent and that's my job when this happens - to be better than the striker I am marking.

Also, I have to be versatile. I don't have a choice who I'm playing against, so I need to be prepared to face anyone, any type of player, and have the ability to do this.

We are a team that tries to win every game and we try to be active in doing that. This is why we need to play with the defence as far up as we do - yes, sometimes it might be difficult but I prefer to play this way because I like attacking football.

So when the defence goes forward, I enjoy it because we want to win and if that means taking this risk, so be it.

When I play right-back, I use my power and pace when I move in front of the midfield and it is important for me when I play as right-back.

JOSE SAYS...

My attacking style is also to do with the team itself - I wouldn't be crazy enough to leave my position to attack without knowing someone would back me up.

The way the team around me plays gives me and the other full-back the opportunity to get forward because I know if I'm further up the field, there will be somebody covering for me.

I can't be in two places at one time, no, but the whole team help each other out by overlapping and covering, allowing us to play the way we do. This way I can find spaces and attack them - that is what I'm always trying to do. So it's like an unwritten rule that both me and Ashley Cole know if one of us goes forward, it is Mikel's job to be there and to cover for us.

It's not something we agree between ourselves or something that just happens on matchdays, but something we work on in training every day because the manager wants to stabilise the team when one of the full-backs goes forward to join an attack.

YURY SAYS...

One of the advantages of playing as a defender when you attack is that you get more space to manoeuvre and decide how you are going to join the attacks, so yes, I can still be a threat going forward.

But, for me, it doesn't matter that much whether I play full-back or left-wing because you still get the chance to join the attacks. But also, in both positions you spend more time doing defensive work when you don't have the ball.

KEEP GOAL *LIKE*

CECH

From shot-stopping to penalty saving, positioning to distribution, Chelsea's number one provides a hands-on approach to keeping the opposition out...

Eye on the ball

Agility

PETR SAYS...

What core skills does a goalkeeper need?

I think it's very important from the start that you have good agility and good coordination because there are plenty of moments in the game where you won't be able to get to the ball without these skills - for example, if the ball takes a deflection.

But the most important thing for a goalkeeper is concentration. If you can focus on every single detail for the whole game, this is the key because then you never get surprised.

You need to read the game, which you will learn from experience. And finally you need a strong mentality because it's hard at the beginning to learn that if you make a mistake, there will be a goal - you have to get used to that if you want to be a goalkeeper.

Reaction saves and one-v-ones

I think you can always read what's going to happen, or
try to read it, in any situation, including one-v-ones. The
key thing is that you can't lose a split second, so you
need to concentrate. If you're ready at any time, then
you have a better chance to control one-v-one
situations, but if you're unprepared mentally and you
suddenly find yourself in a situation, then you might get
surprised - concentration is the key.

You can't lose a
split second so
you always have
to be ready

SKILL TIP...

REFLEXES AND REACTIONS: Agility, quick reactions and reflexes are necessities for goalkeepers. These are improved by training.

One of the most common drills is to practise saving rapid fire shots that make you dive to your left and right for as long as you can.

Using several footballs lined up, get a mate to shoot low to your left then, as you get to your feet as quickly as possible, shoot low to your right and so on. This drill prepares you for match situations where you may need to make a second or third save after initially parrying the ball.

Another exercise involves getting a mate to stand a yard in front of you holding two balls, one in either hand, and throw them at you simultaneously. As he does so he must shout 'left' or 'right' and whichever he shouts is the one you must save.

You should also practise collecting the ball at different heights and in different weather conditions, particularly the wet.

Remember, a good goalkeeper always keeps on his toes so he is ready to react to anything and clutches the ball with 'soft hands,' arms extended and bends his elbows to absorb the pace on the ball.

Be vocal, be dominant, be confident and give defenders clear instructions. It's your box!

Concentration is the key

Look up

Pick out the man

SKILL TIP...

SETTING UP ATTACKS: A goalkeeper can be a valuable source of creating attacks for a team, so it is important to work on your distribution.

As soon as you get hold of the ball, you should be looking to distribute it quickly. Look for a team-mate in space or a team-mate sprinting forward and then try to find him with a long throw or kick. Throwing usually allows for greater accuracy.

However, if there isn't anyone available, then don't simply boot the ball upfield aimlessly, as you'll just hand possession back to your opponents. Always aim for a team-mate.

Practise your kicking and throwing regularly by aiming for a friend in different positions on the halfway line.

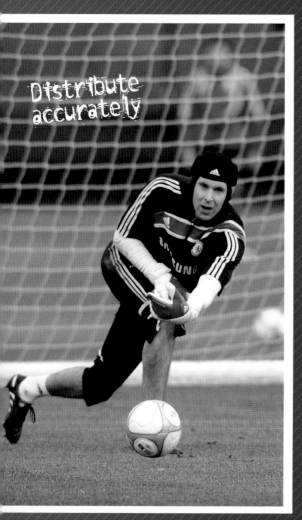

Distribute accurately

Distribution and throwing to launch counter-attacks

We always say at Chelsea that the goalkeeper is the first attacking player as well as the last defender. As soon as he catches the ball, he becomes an attacking player and there are plenty of times when you have the ball as a goalkeeper and you can see space behind the opposition players where there are interesting positions for the counter-attack.

When you see an opportunity like that you have to go for it, so the first thing I do when I catch the ball is always to look upfront to see who's going to be there. You can see if there is a possibility to counter-attack quickly or, if not, what would be the best option to start our own move.

Of course, it needs good movement from your team-mates, who need to be reading the situation as well, because you don't want to kick the ball into a space where it's going to be a ball lost and you have to defend again.

You need to kick and throw the ball a lot in training because you will need to do these things in the games. The best practice is to throw the ball with both arms as well, because sometimes you have an angle of play in front of you with one arm and you need to release the ball quickly and precisely to make it.

So this is what we do every day because it's good for our coordination and also it keeps the balance of your body if you work on both sides.

In training we have different coloured cones in small goals as targets. Someone crosses the ball into us and when we catch the ball he shouts what cone to aim for. We have to look around to see which one of the cones or mini goals we are throwing to - it's the same situation as in a game when you are choosing which player to throw to, so I think it pays off.

As soon as the goalkeeper catches the ball, they become an attacking player

Christoph Lollichon

It helps to have variety in training

On keeping training fresh

Here our goalkeeper coach is Christoph Lollichon, who I worked with when I was at Rennes as well. Everyday he is trying to find something new - new toys, new exercises, whatever. The variety is interesting because you never know what you are going to do in training and that's good. At some places you could arrive in the morning and think, 'I've got to do this, then this, then this' and if it's always the same, you get mentally tired.

But here there's no chance because you never know what is round the corner! But you also see that it's not just by chance, he is not doing these things just to entertain us, he knows exactly where he wants to go and has plans for weeks and months ahead. He knows what he wants to achieve, in the gym, on the pitch, everything.

So I think he is at the top because he has control of everything we, as goalkeepers, will need to do. He knows what we should and shouldn't do and what he should and shouldn't repeat with us. He coordinates with all the physios and doctors as well so if there is a problem, he never asks you to do things that he knows you can't do at that moment.

Clean sheets and vital saves

No matter what the score is at the moment you make a save, it still stops the score changing. If you can stop a team scoring when you're winning 5-4, it is as valuable as at 1-0, it doesn't matter because the most important thing is to help your team win the game.

As the strikers have the target to score goals, goalkeepers have the target not to concede. So when you finish the game with a clean sheet, you know you've done the best you could. But sometimes you concede two goals and you know you've done your best again and could have been man of the match. Of course it's not quite the same because it's always special for a goalkeeper to get a clean sheet. When you have a clean sheet and you win the game as well, this is the top, but important saves come first.

Individual within a team

We're not crazy, just very brave. We have to throw ourselves at people's feet in the six-yard box and it's not easy, but when you make a good save, you get such a rush.

That's why I like being a goalkeeper. I have always liked individual sports like tennis and goalkeeping has its unique, individual aspects, but I prefer team sports because you get a sense of camaraderie and working together towards one goal.

Try to judge the player's body language as he strikes the ball

Facing penalties

You try to read the situation and try to find in the body language of the guy where the penalty might be kicked. You have to try to see what kind of player he is, will he look at you or where he is going to kick it - this goes through your mind before the game and then you try to remember what kind of player he is and what things you've seen him do before.

SKILL TIP...

SAVING PENALTIES: Petr Cech is well accustomed to thinking on the spot, just take his key penalty stop in the 2010 FA Cup Final for example.

Most goalkeepers have different approaches to facing penalties, but there are some general rules to follow, the first being 'always dive'.

There is more chance of saving the ball if you dive and even if it is struck down the middle you may be able to block it.

Most keepers decide which way to dive before the kick is taken. If you know your opponent usually aims for a particular corner, then dive in that direction or, as

a more general rule, right-footed players will aim to the goalkeeper's left and left-footed players to their right. Trust your instincts.

Diving before it is kicked makes it easy for your opponent to send you the wrong way, so you should dive only when the ball is struck. Watching a player's body shape as he strikes the ball can also give you a clue as to where he is going to place it, but looking into his eyes can be deceptive as some players will glance towards one corner then hit it towards the other. If you do save the ball then it is crucial to get back to your feet as quickly as possible to try to save any rebound.

MANAGE *LIKE* ANCELOTTI

You've seen what it takes to become a Chelsea player, but how do you get the best out of them when it matters most? Carlo Ancelotti has a track record of success in management and here's how he does it...

CARLO SAYS...

Play with passion

The most important thing that I say to all my players is to play with passion. I played every game with passion and it is something I look for in a footballer now that I am a manager. You cannot make the most of your ability if you do not have the determination to win every challenge and every game.

It is also important that you have focus and a calm head on the pitch - if you're mentality is correct, you can make the right decisions and this is as important as having technical skills. You can maintain passion and remain mentally calm, it is possible, but usually the passion is a physical thing but this does not mean you need to make bad decisions.

Keep developing yourself

You have to want to improve yourself and your game all the time if you want to develop as a footballer. If you work hard on your strengths and your weaknesses, you will improve as a player and, at the same, develop your physical condition. If you have the desire to improve, then you will become a better player.

Move the ball quickly

The most dangerous time for a team is when they have just lost possession to their opponent. This is the time to attack and attack quickly. When you win the ball back, you must take advantage while the other team is vulnerable and out of position and make the move to their goal as quickly as possible.

This does not mean you have to play a long pass, you must be sensible and think about where the spaces are and who is out of position in the opposition. Look to move the ball between players and attack in numbers so that the defence cannot settle or control the situation. It is harder for a defence to organise itself against a fast counter-attack than against a team that has had possession for 90% of the game.

I call this kind of sudden change of movement from defence to attack 'transition' and it is something I like my teams to see and do whenever there is an opportunity. Obviously it is easier when you have fantastic players like Malouda, Anelka and Drogba in attack because they have the speed and the ability to make space and find the pass at the right moment. But behind them, the midfield and defenders must know when to release the ball in front of them and when to hold onto the ball for ourselves.

This last point is very important. While the counter-attack is dangerous, it is important to know that you must be patient and wait until the right moment to try it. There are times when you must stay calm, play the right pass and not risk possession unless you have the opportunity to start an attack. I like to see quick transition when we attack but I also stress the importance of patience because you cannot always play a pass that will create a chance to score.

After the game

I like to keep my home life and football completely separate, so that I leave my work behind when I go home. It is important to relax and come back to the training ground with a fresh attitude and in a positive mood.

If you win and your team has played well, or after a defeat, I will still watch the game again on video, sometimes twice, to find why we lost or, if we have not lost, what we can improve next time.

This assessment is something you can do for individuals or for a team and, if you do not have video, you can still speak to someone who has been watching about what moments you think need work. You can also learn and improve by watching games and understanding what other teams do in certain situations.

It is important to arrive at training with a positive attitude

Arrigo Sacchi

Sven Goran
Eriksson

Marco van
Basten

Always want to learn

When I finished playing, I worked as a coach with
the national team of Italy when Arrigo Sacchi was
manager. He is famous in Italy for his achievements
as a manager, particularly with AC Milan, where I
played for him alongside some of the best players in
the world – people like Ruud Gullit, Franco Baresi,
Frank Rijkaard and Marco van Basten. He was a
tactical manager and he found new ways of
pressing opponents off the ball and lining his team
up. With the help of some wonderful players, he
won a lot of trophies in Milan.

Working with him as a player and as a young
coach was a wonderful time for me and I think it is
important to learn from intelligent, experienced
men in football. He was not my only influence,
though, I was also able to learn from men like Nils
Liedholm and Sven Goran Eriksson, who coached
me at Roma and taught me the importance of
speaking to your players calmly, even at half-time.

My aim as a manager is to put my ideas across so
that the players understand them and then the
players must implement those ideas on the pitch.
This process is not possible without co-operation,
understanding and mutual respect between coach
and players – you cannot impose ideas.

So there are many different aspects to coaching a
football team, it is not just tactics but it is also not
just about man management - you need to have all
of these skills to achieve success.

Work with good support staff

When I came to Chelsea, I only took with me one member of staff, Bruno Demichelis, and I was joined in my second season by fitness coach Giovanni Mauri. Apart from them, I decided to work with the people already here at the club and they have all been fantastic. Ray Wilkins, Paul Clement, Christophe Lollichon and all the backroom staff here have all helped me a lot since I arrived. A manager needs to have the support of talented and intelligent coaches who can offer advice and also discuss with him the games. It also helped me that Ray was once an AC Milan player as well and has a wonderful knowledge of the game and of Italian!

Carlo with Ray Wilkins (centre) and Giovanni Mauri

THINK LIKE
CHELSEA FC

A player's talent is the thing that comes first and foremost in everyone's mind with a young footballer, but, as Chelsea assistant manager Ray Wilkins explains, there are so many more things that you need to have in your armoury to achieve greatness or to achieve status as a Premier League footballer...

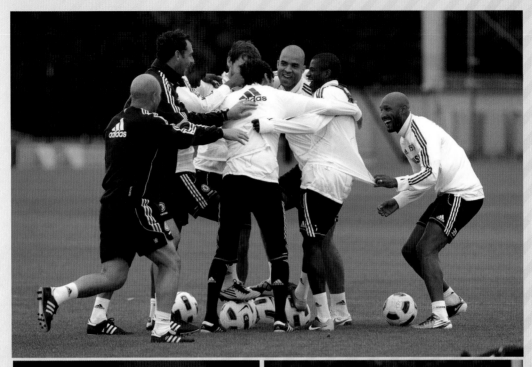

Dedication is paramount

You've got to love the game. I honestly believe if you're going to do something in life, and you want to do it wonderfully well, you have to love what you're doing - if you don't love it, leave it.

When I was growing up, I loved football and I wanted to play the game every minute of the day. I really do believe that is necessary because if you want to be a professional footballer but you don't want to give it 100 per cent, then leave it alone, because there's someone else that will.

Decision-making on the pitch

The ability to make the right decisions on the pitch comes from a number of factors, especially the advice we, as coaches, give players right the way through their development. If they take on board the advice we try to give them, then they're on the right road.

More often than not, we've discovered that, under pressure a player will revert back to the first thing they were taught. We hope that, by coaching what we think is the right way of playing into players from a young age, that will be what they revert back to in times of pressure.

If a player is taught at his first side to hit the ball long, from back to front, and then joins a club that wants to play the ball into midfield, when he's having a bad time he will quite likely revert back to what he knows and send the ball long.

Hopefully we're bringing our players up to pass the ball and play through midfield, so whenever they have a problem, they'll play simply and knock the ball into midfield – that way we'll get it right as a team and as individuals. All great players do the simple things correctly.

Keep calm when you're struggling

As a midfield player, if you've missed five passes and are worried, then play a simple pass next time you get the ball and know you're playing well again. Don't do anything outrageous if you've missed a few passes, just get back to doing things right.

For a striker who's missed a few chances on the trot, the important thing is that you keep getting in the right positions to miss the chances in the first place. Whether you've missed five or not, go back in there and miss another one if need be, but the seventh one will go in. Make sure, if things are going wrong, you go back and make another pass, or take another chance.

Use disappointment to your advantage

It's not easy for prospective footballers because there are disappointments right the way along the line. So we all have disappointments, but it's how you react to it that matters. You have to react to those disappointments in the most positive fashion you possibly can and keep going for it.

We're all going to get down at some point, that's a fact of life, but it's about coming back and presenting yourself once again, it's important to realise that.

Somewhere along the line, we're all guilty of mollycoddling young talent and sometimes they need to see that disappointment and come good again after it, react to it positively.

Try to avoid complacency

It's down to us as coaches to notice if a player starts coasting or is getting complacent. It can come from within the player to think that it's all very simple and it's up to us to make sure he does things properly.

Work on weaknesses and strengths

Perhaps training on the same things over and over again can get monotonous, but then monotony can sometimes bring brilliance as well and that's what we're looking for. We're looking for the guy that can reproduce his form day in, day out.

I'll watch Frank Lampard in training and he works so hard on his skills, he doesn't want anything simple. He doesn't want a ball that's played in quite pleasantly to his feet, he wants one that bounces and skips up in front of him so he can react to it and try to make something happen from it.

That's what makes him the player he is, because when he gets into the box and the ball comes into him, he's ready, he's gone past his defender and the ball's in the back of the net.

This is what makes these guys the best - they have to keep working, not only on their deficiencies, but on what they're already good at.

GOOD LUCK

Now you have seen what we do at Chelsea, I hope you will be inspired to go out and continue to develop as a footballer. All the things we do at this club, which are included in this book, will help you to improve your game and your physical condition as an athlete.

I have one final piece of advice for every young player. Do not compare yourself with other players because every person is born with different abilities and skills.

You can only improve your own levels and stretch your own limits – if you try to be like somebody else you will not be developing your strengths, but theirs. Remember this and make the most of your abilities.

get closer

Get closer to ticket access
Get closer to behind-the-scenes information
Get closer to exclusive member offers & discounts

Be more than just a fan. **Be True Blue**.